All Glories to Śrī



# The Search For Śrī Krishna

## Reality The Beautiful

**līlā premṇā priyādhikyaṁ**
**mādhuryaṁ veṇu-rūpayoḥ**
**ity asādhāraṇaṁ proktaṁ**
**govindasya catuṣṭayam**

Krishna has four superexcellent qualities: His wonderful pastimes, His wonderful associates like the *gopīs*, who are very dear to Him, His sweet beauty, and the sweet vibration of His flute.

(*Chaitanya-caritāmṛta Madhya-līlā* 23.84)

# The Search For Śrī Krishna

## Reality The Beautiful

Through His holy name, transcendental sound preached and practiced by Śrī Chaitanyadeva, who is none other than Rādhā and Govinda combined — and propagated by Śrīla Bhaktisiddhānta Saraswatī Ṭhākur


His divine Grace

**Srila Bhakti Raksak Sridhar Dev-Goswami Maharaj**



Śrī Chaitanya Sāraswat Maṭh

First Printing 1983 5,000 copies
Second Printing 1983 5.000 copies
Third Printing 1986 3,000 copies
Fourth Printing 1988 5,000 copies
Fifth Printing 2000 2,500 copies

Published by Vaishnava Seva Society
P.O. Box 8040
Santa Cruz, California 95061
(831) 462-4712
www.SevaAshram.com

Special thanks to the following devotees for their help with this current edition: Swami B.P. Janardan, Swami B.C. Parvat, Navadwip Prabhu, Sarvabhavana Prabhu, Ananta Krishna Prabhu, Tilak devi dasi, Dayal Dulal Prabhu.

# Contents

President-Āchārya Śrī Chaitanya Sāraswat Maṭh
Śrīla Bhakti Sundar Govinda Dev-Goswāmī Mahārāj

Founder-Āchārya Śrī Chaitanya Sāraswat Maṭh
Śrīla Bhakti Rakṣak Śrīdhar Dev-Goswāmī Mahārāj

Śrīla Bhaktisiddhānta Saraswatī Ṭhākur

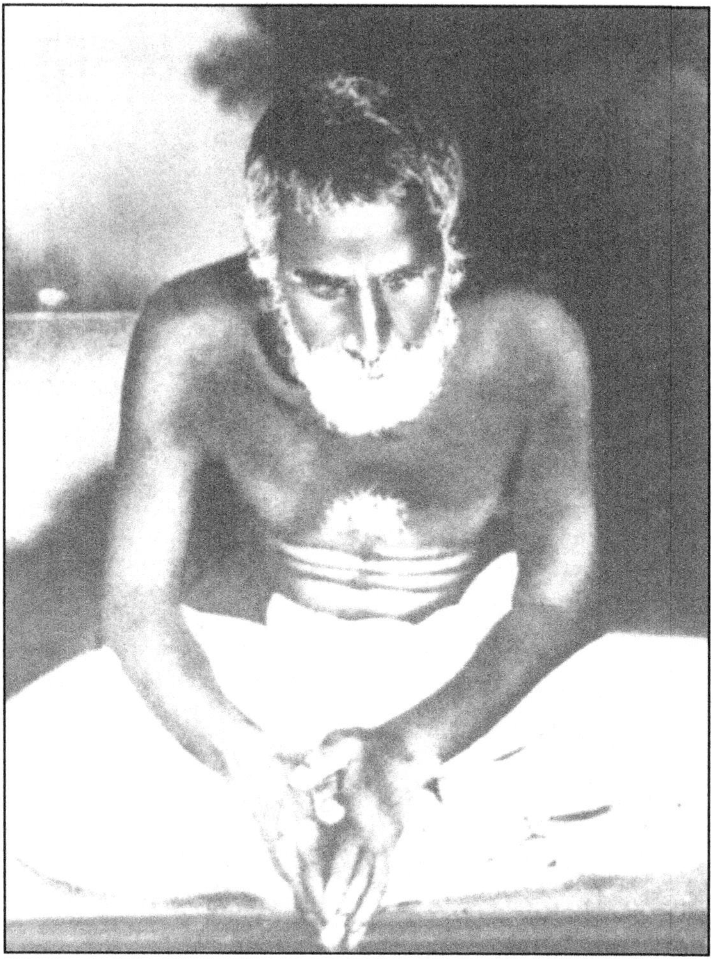

Śrīla Gaura Kiśora Dāsa Bābājī Mahārāj

Śrīla Bhaktivinoda Ṭhākur

# FOREWORD

by

**Śrīla Bhaktivinoda Ṭhākur**

Nineteenth Century Founder of the Krishna Consciousness Movement

We love to read a book which we have never read before. We are anxious to gather whatever information is contained in it, and with such acquirement our curiosity stops. This mode of study prevails amongst

"Party spirit—that great enemy of truth—will always baffle the attempt of the inquirer who tries to gather truth from the religious works of his nation and will make him believe that the Absolute Truth is nowhere except in his old religious book."

*Śrīla Bhaktivinoda Ṭhākur*

a great number of readers who are great men in their own estimation as well as in the estimation of those who are of their own stamp. In fact, most readers are mere repositories of facts and statements made by other people. But this is not study. The student is to read the facts with a view to create, and not with the object of fruitless retention. Students, like satellites, should reflect whatever light they receive from authors, and not imprison the facts and thoughts just as the magistrates imprison the convicts in the jail!

Thought is progressive. The author's thought must have progress in the reader in the shape of correction or development. He is the best critic who can show the further development of an old thought; but a mere denouncer is the enemy of progress, and consequently of nature. Progress certainly is the law of nature, and there must be corrections and developments with the progress of time. But progress means going further or rising higher. The shallow critic and the fruitless reader are the two great enemies of progress. We must shun them.

The true critic, on the other hand, advises us to preserve what we have already obtained, and to adjust our race from that point where we have arrived in the heat of our progress. He will never advise us to go back to the point whence we started, as he fully knows that in that case there will be a fruitless loss of our valuable time and labor. He will direct the adjustment of the angle of our race at the point where we are.

This is also the characteristic of the useful student. He will read an old author and will find out his exact position in the progress of thought. He will never propose to burn a book on the ground that it contains thoughts which are useless. No thought is useless. Thoughts are means by which we attain our objects. The reader who denounces a bad thought does not know that a bad road is even capable of improvement and conversion into a good one. One thought is a road leading to another. Thus, the reader will find that one thought, which is the object today, will be the means of a further object tomorrow. Thoughts will necessarily continue to be an endless series of means and objects in the progress of humanity.

The great reformers will always assert that they have come out not to *destroy* the old law, but to *fulfill* it. Valmiki, Vyāsa, Plato, Jesus, Mohammed, Confucius, and Chaitanya Mahāprabhu assert the fact either expressly or by their conduct.

Our critic, however, may nobly tell us that a reformer like Vyāsa, unless purely explained, may lead thousands of men into great trouble in time to come. But dear critic! Study the history of ages and countries! Where have you found the philosopher and reformer fully understood by the people? The popular religion is fear of God, and not the pure spiritual love which Plato, Vyāsa, Jesus, and Chaitanya taught to their respective peoples! Whether you give the absolute religion in figures or simple expressions, or teach them by means of books or oral speeches, the ignorant and the thoughtless must degrade it.

It is indeed very easy to tell, and swift to hear, that Absolute Truth has such an affinity with the human soul that it comes through as if intuitively, and that no exertion is necessary to teach the precepts of true religion, but this is a deceptive idea. It may be true of ethics and of the alphabet of religion, but not of the highest form of faith, which requires an exalted soul to understand. All higher truths, though intuitive, require previous education in the simpler ones. That religion is the purest which gives us the purest idea of God. How then is it possible that the ignorant will ever obtain the absolute religion, as long as they are ignorant?

So we are not to scandalize the Savior of Jerusalem or the Savior of Nadia for these subsequent evils. Luthers, instead of critics, are what we want for the correction of those evils by the true interpretation of the original precepts.

God gives us truth as He gave it to Vyāsa, when we earnestly seek for it. Truth is eternal and inexhaustable. The soul receives a revelation when it is anxious for it. The souls of the great thinkers of the bygone ages, who now live spiritually, often approach our inquiring spirit and assist it in its development. Thus, Vyāsa was assisted by Nārada and Brahmā. Our *śāstras*, or in other words, books of thought, do not contain all that we could get from the infinite Father. No book is without its errors. God's revelation is Absolute Truth, but it is scarcely received and preserved in its natural purity. We have been advised in the *Śrīmad-Bhāgavatam* (11.14.3) to believe that truth when revealed is absolute, but it gets the tincture of the nature of the receiver in course of time, and is converted into error by continual exchange of hands from age to age. New revelations, therefore, are continually necessary in order to keep truth in its original purity. We are thus warned to be careful in our studies of old authors, however wise they are reputed to be. Here, we have full liberty to reject the wrong idea, which is not sanctioned by the peace of conscience.

Vyāsa was not satisfied with what he collected in the *Vedas*, arranged in the *Purāṇas*, and composed in the *Mahābhārata*. The peace of his conscience did not sanction his labors. It told him from inside, "No, Vyāsa! You can't rest contented with the erroneous picture of truth which was necessarily presented to you by the sages of bygone days! You must yourself knock at the door of the inexhaustible store of truth from which the former sages drew their wealth. Go! Go up to the fountainhead of truth, where no pilgrim meets with disappointment of any kind. Vyāsa did it and obtained what he wanted. We have all been advised to do so.

Liberty then, is the principle which we must consider as the most valuable gift of God. We must not allow ourselves to be led by those who lived and thought before us. We must think for ourselves and try to get further truths, which are still undiscovered. In the *Śrīmad Bhāgavatam* (11.21.23) we have been advised to take the spirit of the *śāstras*, and not the words. The *Bhāgavata* is therefore a religion of liberty, unmixed truth, and absolute love.

The other characteristic is progress. Liberty certainly is the father of all progress. Holy liberty is the cause of progress upwards and upwards in eternity and endless activity of love. Liberty misused causes degradation, and the *Vaiṣṇava* must always carefully use this high and beautiful gift of God.

The spirit of this text goes far to honor all great reformers and teachers who lived and will live in other countries. The *Vaiṣṇava* is ready to honor all men without distinction of caste, because they are filled with the energy of God. See how universal is the religion of the *Bhāgavata*. It is not intended for a certain class of Hindus alone, but it is a gift to man at large, in whatever country he is born, and in whatever society he is bred. In short, *Vaiṣṇavism* is the Absolute Love binding all men together into the infinite unconditioned and absolute God. May peace reign forever in the whole universe in the continual development of its purity by the exertion of the future heroes, who will be blessed according to the promise of the *Bhāgavata* with powers from the Almighty Father, the Creator, Preserver, and the Annihilator of all things in Heaven and Earth.

—*From an English lecture delivered in 1869, at Dinajpur, West Bengal.*

Śrīla Bhaktivedanta Swāmī Prabhupād and Śrīla Srīdhar Mahārāj sharing the vyāsāsana, the seat of Vyāsa offered to the *bona fide* spiritual master. [Śrīla Govinda Mahārāj (near the microphone) is speaking.]

# PREFACE

by
**Śrīla Bhaktivedanta Swāmī Prabhupād**
Founder-Āchārya of the International Society for Krishna Consciousness

We are very fortunate to hear His Divine Grace, Om Viṣṇupāda Paramahaṁsa Parivrajak Āchārya Bhakti Rakṣak Śrīdhar Mahārāj. By age and by experience, in both ways, he is senior to me. I was fortunate to have his association since a long time, since perhaps 1930. At that time he had not accepted *sannyās*, but had just left home. He went to preach in Allahabad, and on that auspicious occasion we were connected.

Śrīdhar Mahārāj lived in my house for many years, so naturally we had very intimate talks. He has such high realizations of Krishna that one would faint to hear them. He was always my good advisor, and I took his advice very seriously because from the very beginning I knew that he was a pure devotee of Krishna. So, I wanted to associate with him. Krishna and Prabhupād, Śrīla Bhaktisiddhānta Saraswati Ṭhākur, liked him to prepare me. Our relationship is very intimate.

After the breakdown of our spiritual master's institution I wanted to organize another institution making

Śrīdhar Mahārāj the head. Śrīla Bhaktisiddhānta Saraswati Ṭhākur told me that Śrīdhar Mahārāj is one of the finest preachers of Krishna consciousness in the world, so I wanted to take him everywhere. This was my earnest desire. But since he could not go around the world and preach, at least the people of the world should come to hear from him.

For spiritual advancement of life we must go to someone who is actually practicing spiritual life. So if one is actually serious to take instructions from a *śikṣa guru*, or instructing spiritual master, I can refer him to one who is the most competent of all my Godbrothers. This is B.R. Śrīdhar Mahārāj. I consider Śrīdhar Mahārāj to be even my *śikṣa guru*, so what to speak of the benefit that others can have from his association.

# INTRODUCTION

Everyone is searching for *rasa*, pleasure. The status of *rasa is* the highest. As persons we have our subjective existence, but *rasa*, pleasure, has His supersubjective existence. He is a person. He is *akhila rasāmṛta-mūrtiḥ*: the reservoir of all pleasure. He is Krishna. *Rasa* is Krishna. There cannot be *rasa* in any other place but Krishna. He is the fountainhead of all different types of *rasa*. So, by the nature of our constitution we have to search after Krishna.

In the *Brahma-sūtra* it is said, "Inquire after the supreme cause of this world. Search!" From where has everything come? How is everything maintaining its existence? By whom? And ultimately, where does everything enter after death? That is *brahma*, spirit, the most fundamental plane from where everything springs up, remains, and ultimately enters.

Where is *brahma*? The *Brahma-sūtra* advises us to inquire after the prime cause, the biggest, the all-accommodating. But Śrī Chaitanya Mahāprabhu replaced that, *Śrīmad-Bhāgavatam* replaced that with *Kṛṣṇānusandhāna*: the search for Śrī Krishna.

*Brahmā-jijñāsā*, the search for spirit, is a dry thing. That is only the exercise of your thinking faculty, a jugglery of reason. Leave that behind. Begin the search for Śrī Krishna and quench the thirst of your heart. *Rasa jijñāsā, raso vai saḥ*. The things acquired by your reason won't satisfy you. *Jñāna*, knowledge, cannot really quench your thirst, so instead of *brahma-jijñāsā* accept *Kṛṣṇānusandhāna* and begin the search for Śrī Krishna.

Where is Krishna? Our real want will be satisfied only by getting the service of Krishna; not by anything else. We want to satisfy the innermost demands of our hearts. We don't care to know where we are or what is controlling everything, but we really want to quench our thirst for *rasa*, for *mādhurya*, for sweetness. We must search neither for knowledge nor for the controller of this world; we must search after *rasa*, *ānandam*, after beauty and charm.

Śrī Chaitanya Mahāprabhu and *Śrīmad-Bhāgavatam* have taught us what to beg for, what to pray for, what to want. They have taught us, "If you beg, beg for Krishna, not for anything else." So, the fate of the *Vaiṣṇavas*, the students of the *Bhāgavata* and the followers of Mahāprabhu, is sealed in the search for Śrī Krishna. We want nothing else but Krishna.

The *Vedas* say, *sṛṇvantu viśve amṛtasya putrāḥ*: "O, you sons of nectar, sons of the nectarine ocean sea: please listen to me. You were born in nectar; you were born to taste nectar, and you must not allow yourselves to be satisfied by anything but nectar. So, however misguided you may be for the time being, awake! Arise! Search for that nectar, that satisfaction." The *Vedas* tell us, "*Oṁ*!" *Oṁ* means a big "Yes!" "What you are searching for, that is! Don't be disappointed." The *Vedas* say that the object of our inner search exists. The common search of all your hearts *is* existing, and your thirst *will* be quenched. By your constitution you are meant for that and you deserve that, so don't be afraid; don't be cowed down. It is already given in your being. And you can never be satisfied with anything else. So prepare yourself, after your long search, to receive that long missing nectar in its full form and quality. Awake! Arise! Search for your fortune and you cannot but have that. It is your birthright. It is the wealth of your own soul. It cannot but be within you. You have no other business, no other engagement but *Kṛṣṇānusandhāna*, the Search for Śrī Krishna: Reality the Beautiful.

# Krishna Consciousness: Love and Beauty

At the beginning of the twentieth century, the Bengali poet Hemachandra wrote, "There are so many countries rising in prominence: this land, that land. Japan is a very small country, but it is rising like the sun. Only India is under eternal slumber." When he mentioned the other part of the world, he said, "America is rising forcefully, as if he is coming to swallow the whole world. Sometimes he is shouting as if with a war cry, and the whole world is shivering. His enthusiasm is so intense and great that he wants to snatch the world from the solar system, and give it a new shape, a new molding." America has been mentioned in this way by Hemachandra. In the same way, Bhaktivedanta Swāmī Mahārāj came to give the world a new shape through Krishna consciousness. He once said, "We must go there and build it in a new way—with Krishna consciousness."

What is Krishna consciousness? Krishna consciousness means real love and beauty. Real love and beauty must predominate; not selfishness, or exploitation. Generally, whenever we see beauty, we think that beauty is to be exploited, but actually, beauty is the exploiter, beauty is the master, and beauty is the controlling principle.

And what is love? Love means sacrifice for others. We should not think that sacrifice is to be exploited by us. Who is to be the recipient of sacrifice? Is it our party? No. We are in the group of those who sacrifice themselves: the predominated negative party, Mahābhāva's party. The underlying principle of love is sacrifice, but sacrifice for whom? And who is the beneficiary? Love is the beneficiary. Everyone should contribute to the center, but no one should draw energy from there. "Die to live." With this spirit we should combine and work for real love and beauty.

## BANNER OF LOVE

And beauty will be victorious in the world. Love will be victorious in the world. We will sacrifice everything to see that the banner of divine love will flutter all over the world, for a particle of that divine love will be able to keep peace and distribute peace in all directions. Just as fighting soldiers dedicate everything, and give their lives so their countrymen will benefit in the future, we should sacrifice our lives and work to bring real peace for everyone.

In Vṛndāvana, the land of Krishna, the standard of sacrifice is unlimited. Devotees there are willing to risk everything for Krishna. If that principle of sacrifice is enthroned, then peace will automatically follow.

Krishna consciousness should be enthroned above all other conceptions. All other conceptions are meant to be subservient to Krishna consciousness. The ideal of Vṛndāvana, Krishna's abode, is above all other ideals. In theistic comparison, the conception of Śrī Chaitanya Mahāprabhu's *līlā* is above all other conceptions. There, theism reaches its zenith. That is our highest goal, and step by step, that should be explained, thought out, accepted, and preached.

## ATOMIC DEATH

Without this, what sort of benefit are you expecting from your present engagement? Only death is awaiting you. You are so proud of this scientific civilization and are boasting so much, but death is awaiting you whether it is atomic death or natural death. You can't cross death. One English poet has written:

> **The boast of heraldry, the pomp of power,**
> **And all that beauty, all that wealth e'er gave**
> **Awaits alike the inevitable hour:**
> **The paths of glory lead but to the grave**
>
> —Thomas Gray's *Elegy in a Country Churchyard*

You do not care to solve the greatest danger. You say that you are big thinkers, that you are great men, and that you should command the respect of society, but the general inevitable problem for every atom here is death. What is your contribution for solving the greatest danger which is waiting to devour everyone—scientist, insect, or virus? What is your solution to death? Have you taken any steps to solve that universal danger? What you are doing at present is exploitation, and you are encouraging a lower life as a reaction. You are exploiting nature, and everyone who is deriving the benefits will have to pay to the farthing with interest.

"For every action there is an equal and opposite reaction." This is your statement, but what have you done to solve that? You are endangering the fate of the world by your fascinating proposals of apparent comfort. What is this? You are avoiding the greatest inevitable danger, so your life is a useless malengagement. In one sense, you are traitors to society. Come with courage to face and solve the real problem, the common problem, and the most dangerous problem; otherwise you should leave the field and go away. Leave it to us. We shall prove that the world is an abode of perfect happiness: *(viśvaṁ pūrṇa sukhāyate)*.

## DIVE DEEP INTO REALITY

But to understand this, you will have to dive deep, not into the plane of body and mind, but into the plane of soul. You will have to dive deep into the reality that is within us. It is not a foreign thing to be acquired by loan, but the soul is within everyone, even the insects and the trees. So, we have to rise to the plane of soul. Eliminate both your physical and mental encasements and find out your own self. There you

A sixteenth century painting of Śrī Chaitanya Mahāprabhu and His associates discussing *Śrīmad-Bhāgavatam*.

will find the key, the clue to the proper world where life is worth living.

The solution is there; a hint is given by many *mahājanas*, by great saints in every religious sect to some extent, but our claim is that India has given the highest conception of the spiritual world in the *Bhagavad-gītā* and *Śrīmad-Bhāgavatam*. So, we challenge all of you: we are not imaginationists; we are most practical thinkers. We don't avoid any great problem by saying, "Oh, it can't be solved." We do not belong to the party that wants to easily take prestige and fame. We don't want to classify ourselves with those hoaxing people. Come and see whether the plane of reality can be found. You are not required to spend any less energy in your campaign, so take our program; try it and see.

Where are you? Who are you? What is the real nature of the world? In the *Koran*, in the *Bible*, and in the *Vedas*, and in every other scripture, a hope and hint has been given about the life of reality. Is this all a hoax? What charm have the materialists given? That charm is only for the self-deceivers, and that is dragging them into the country of loan and debt, the land where "Every action has an equal and opposite reaction." So, a divine civilization should be drawn out into this plane. We have to try the path that has been suggested by the great saints and scriptures. It is not unreasonable. It is not madness. Come, reason can also be applied there.

Śrī Chaitanya Mahāprabhu gave a solution to all our problems with an allegorical example. He said, "We see that you are poor, but there is a happy solution. Your wealth is underground in your own room: just try to unearth it. Don't approach it from the southern side, the give-and-take method of *karma*, for then whatever you do will bring some reaction that will capture and disturb you, and you will have no time to reach the proper solution. If you approach that hidden wealth from the western side, through the *yoga* system, by manipulating the subtle forces of nature to attain supernatural mystic power, that will enchant you and take your attention away from the desired goal. Your own activity in the wrong direction will create obstacles to your achievement.

## THE SAMĀDHI PHANTOM

"If you approach the treasure from the north, the side of that grand *brahmāsmi*, the impersonal conception, with the help of misinterpreted Vedantic logic, then you will enter into eternal *samādhi*, that great phantom will swallow you up, your existence will be nowhere, and who will come to enjoy the peace of getting the wealth? Only if you approach from the eastern side, with the help of devotion, will you get the wealth easily. That is the direction of the sunrise, the light giving direction. And that light is not prepared by our own hand; that light is from the source of all light: the revealed truth. It is extended from the quarter which is unknown to us. That light is revealed knowledge, *bhakti*, the path of devotion.

Adopt that path in your search for the real wealth within you, and easily you will find your own self, which is most wonderful *(āścaryavat paśyati kaścid enam)*. Discovering that your own self is so wonderful, you will be ashamed, thinking, "How could I have been carried away by the charm of this mundane world? I am the soul. How was it possible for *māyā* to have such enchanting power over me that my own self, which is so wonderful and so valuable, was drawn into illusion? The peace which is within me has been greatly admired by the spiritual stalwarts, but I have come in connection with mortal and nasty, rotten things. How? It is most wonderful, but I was deceived."

Then from *ātmā* to Paramātmā, from soul to Supersoul, then from Vāsudeva to Nārāyaṇa, and then from Nārāyaṇa to Krishna, the progressive understanding in God realization is not unscientific; it is really scientific. This is *vijñāna*, scientific knowledge:

**jñānaṁ te 'haṁ sa-vijñānam**
**idaṁ vakṣyāmy aśeṣataḥ**
**yaj jñātvā neha bhūyo 'nyaj**
**jñātavyam avaśiṣyate**

In the *Bhagavad-gītā* (7.2) Krishna says, "Arjuna, now I shall explain to you scientific knowledge not only about the soul, but also about its potency. The mind, the senses, and the modes of nature are all *non-ātmā*, or material. There is a direct and indirect approach towards reality which I shall now explain to you. Please listen attentively to Me: *jñānaṁ te' ham sa-vijñānam*. What is this? There is Myself and My potency, and the *jīva*, the living entity, is the marginal potency which is filling up all these material worlds." If the *jīva-śakti*, the spiritual potency, were withdrawn, then everything would be stone, and who would care for exploitation? All this fighting tendency, this tendency for exploitation would stop if the marginal potency, the *jīva*, were withdrawn from matter. Everything would be dead. The soul has entered into this material consciousness and has made it a moving thing. You should understand this properly, in a scientific way. We are not lacking in our ability to give you a scientific explanation.

### PLANE OF SELF-DECEPTION

A higher conception of the finer world is here. It is real, and where you are trying your utmost to make a stand, the place that you consider real is unreal.

**yā niśā sarva-bhūtānāṁ**
**tasyāṁ jāgarti saṁyamī**
**yasyāṁ jāgrati bhūtāni**
**sā niśā paśyato muneḥ**

—*Bhagavad-gītā* (2.69)

"You are asleep to your real self-interest and the real truth, while you are awake in the plane of self-deception." We must establish ourselves in the plane of reality, and try our best to extend it to others.

And to preach means this: "I sincerely have faith in Krishna consciousness and relish it to the utmost. I find that my future prospect is also here. Because I feel that it is very tasteful, useful, and wholesome, I have come to distribute it to you, my friends. We should guide our lives according to the principles of Krishna consciousness as taught by the spiritual master. Take it, and you will be successful in fulfilling the goal of your life."

## RASA, HAPPINESS, ECSTASY

In this way, we have to approach everyone with God consciousness, Krishna consciousness. We must show how God consciousness ultimately merges in Krishna consciousness. We have to prove dexterously, step by step, that Krishna is the reservoir of all pleasure (*akhila rasāmṛta mūrtiḥ*). What is Krishna consciousness? Rūpa Goswāmī has given a scientific definition. *Rasa*, pleasure, cannot be avoided. We are all after *rasa*. Everyone, every unit, even the smallest unit of the world is always hankering after *rasa*, happiness, ecstasy, and all possible phases of *rasa* are personified in Krishna. Try to understand how it is. What is *rasa*? What is its nature? How can a comparison in *rasa* be drawn? In this way, step by step, you will have to come to the Krishna conception of Godhead. It is not a tale from the ancient Indian scriptures. Krishna is not the object of a tale, but fact. You have to come out and face that living fact, that reality. We shall try our best to show you how it can be a fact. Krishna is a fact. He is a reality, and reality is for itself.

You have to pay for the goal. You must "Die to live," and in this way you will feel that it is not a hoax. When you progress on the path, you will feel it (*bhaktiḥ pareśānubhavo viraktir anyatra ca*). With every step forward, you will feel these three things: satisfaction, nourishment, and the eradication of your hunger. Your hankering in general will be diminished.

Generally, we feel, "I want this, I want that, I want everything; still I have not satisfied my hunger." But you will feel that your hunger is being appeased as you progress in Krishna consciousness, and what you previously thought would give you relief will take leave from you automatically. Their trade won't continue; they will all withdraw, your natural inclination for spiritual advancement will automatically increase, and you will find acceleration in your progress. "You will practically feel these three things, so come and take what we say." In this way, you have to approach one and all, leaving the result to the Lord.

## FRUITS OF ENERGY

We are only agents, and we are working because He has ordered us, so we must remember what is *bhakti*, what is devotion proper. Whatever I do, the wage I earn must not come to me; I am only an agent. The benefit should go to the proprietor, to my master, Krishna. We should move with this idea, and that will be *bhakti* proper. Otherwise, we will be engaged in *karma-kānda*: fruit-hunting. I want to enjoy the result of *karma* for myself, but the result should go to my master. I am His servant, and I am working under His order. I am His slave; I am not the proprietor. I am not the proper person to be the recipient of the fruits of energy. The master of energy is the Supreme Lord, and all the products of energy should go to Him. It must not be tampered with on the way. This should be the attitude of every worker. Then it will be *bhakti* proper. We are not the recipients; He is the recipient. We must always be conscious that the only beneficiary is He. Only then are we devotees. We are not the beneficiaries, but selfless workers. It is said in the *Bhagavad-gītā* (2.47):

**karmaṇy evādhikāras te**
**mā phaleṣu kadācana**
**mā karma-phala-hetur bhūr**
**mā te saṅgo 'stv akarmaṇi**

"You have a right to perform your duty, but you have no right to enjoy the fruits of your work." This is a great warning. Krishna says, "Do not think that because you are not the beneficiary of the fruits of your action, you have no reason to take so much trouble to work—never." That is the most heinous curse, to think that because I am not the beneficiary, I am not going to work. Even selfless activity is also of a lower order. Rather we must perform godly activity for the satisfaction of the Supreme Lord. That is *bhakti*, or devotion. And there is also a gradation in *bhakti*: there is a big division between *vidhi-bhakti* and *rāga-bhakti*, calculative devotion and spontaneous devotion.

## AUTOCRAT, DESPOT, AND LIAR

God is not a constitutional king, but He is an autocrat. To work for an autocrat is the highest conception of sacrifice. What degree of selflessness and courage is required to work for an autocrat, a despot, a liar who is up to anything? Not only that, His normal position is such. It is not a temporary temperament, but His eternal inner nature. Krishna is an autocrat because law emanates from Him. An autocrat is above law. When there are many, there is a need for law; when there is only one, there is no need for law. Krishna is a despot, but He is absolute good. If there is any check in His despotism, the world will be the loser. Goodness must have its full flow. Is that bad? Can there be any objection to this? Goodness must have its freedom to flow anywhere and everywhere. If we say that God is absolute good, then what do we lose by giving Him autocracy? Should autocracy be with the ignorant and the fools? No. The absolute good must have full autocracy. Not that law will go to bind His hands. Then we will be losers. And Krishna is a liar, to entice us, because we cannot understand the whole truth. So to entice us to gradually come to the truth, He has become a liar.

The first thing to understand is that He is all goodness, so everything emanating from Him cannot but be good. Any defect is on our side. We are encroachers. He is not an encroacher. But He shows this as His play, *līlā*. Everything belongs to Him, so there is no lying. When He says, "Let there be light," there was light: "Let there be water," there was water. If He has such potential power, can there be any lying there?

We have to sacrifice ourselves for Krishna, because He is the absolute good, beauty, and love. Faith and selflessness are required to such a high degree. If we accept Krishna consciousness as our highest ideal, then so much sacrifice is necessary, but sacrifice means life: "Die to live." There is no loss by sacrifice. We can only gain by giving ourselves.

So, *kīrtan*, or preaching has been accepted as the means to the end. There are so many ways by which we can approach the souls of this world with *kīrtan*: by direct approach, through books, and by performing *saṅkīrtan*, chanting the holy name congregationally. By helping others, we help ourselves: we help our own fortune and our own faith. Not only will others benefit by our performance of *kīrtan*, but we will also benefit eternally.

## ETERNAL VACUUM

Krishna says in *Bhagavad-gītā* (2.47), "Never be attached to not doing your duty *(mā te saṅgo 'stv akarmaṇi)*. Because you are required to work for Me, will you stop work? Don't subject yourself to that painful reaction, for then you will be doomed. Don't be attached to stop work and strike. No. That is a dangerous vacuum. Don't jump there in that eternal vacuum, but work for Me, and you will thrive." Krishna says, "Abandon all varieties of duty, and just surrender unto Me *(sarva dharmān parityajya mām ekaṁ śaraṇaṁ vraja)*. My position is such: I am your guardian, your friend, your everything. Your goal of life is to be found in Me. Believe it Arjuna. At least I must not deceive

As Śrī Chaitanya, Lord Krishna came to preach about Himself.

you. You are my friend—You can take it for certain."

**man-manā bhava mad-bhakto**
**mad-yājī māṁ namaskuru**
**mām evaiṣyasi satyaṁ te**
**pratijāne priyo 'si me**

—*Bhagavad-gītā* (18.65)

"Think of Me always, and become My devotee. Worship Me, and bow down before Me. In this way you will certainly come to Me. My dear friend, I promise you on oath, I am speaking the truth. I am everything. Try to come to Me. I am the goal, the fulfillment of life not only for you, but for everyone. From the absolute consideration My position is such. At least you are My friend. I won't deceive you. You can believe Me. I promise that I am so."

How shamelessly Krishna is expressing Himself here. He has come to plead for Himself so much, for our benefit. And a record is kept in the *Bhagavad-gītā* for our guidance. And Lord Krishna came as Śrī Chaitanya Mahāprabhu to preach about Himself. He came as His own canvasser with His eternal associates. He even brought *Śrīmatī* Rādhārāṇī, devotion personified, along with Him, saying, "I will show how charming Your position in My service is, how beautiful and dignified the devotion of My other half can be. So, come along with Me." And Baladeva has come as Nityānanda to canvass, and Vṛndāvana has come to canvass itself in Navadwīpa. So we are most indebted to the canvasser, especially when Krishna Himself has come to canvass and to show how beautiful, how magnanimous, and how sacrificing divine love is.

# Saints, Scriptures, and Gurus

*The purpose of pilgrimage is to hear from the saintly persons residing in a holy place. The following is a conversation with* Śrīla Śrīdhar *Mahārāj and three European students searching India for truth.*

**Śrīdhar Mahārāj:** Why have you come to India?
**Student:** For pilgrimage. We came to visit the holy places like Navadwīpa, Vṛndāvana, and Jagannātha Purī. That was the main reason we came to India.
**Śrīdhar Mahārāj:** How have you come to know all these things? By books?
**Student:** Yes, by the books of Śrīla Prabhupād.
**Śrīdhar Mahārāj:** What book?
**Student:** *Bhagavad-gītā.*
**Śrīdhar Mahārāj:** Oh. The *Bhagavad-gītā As It Is* by Bhaktivedanta Swāmī Mahārāj.
**Student:** Yes.

## Bhagavad-gītā: "Cure Thyself"

**Śrīdhar Mahārāj:** Many years ago, a German scholar expressed his opinion that *Bhagavad-gītā* is the highest spiritual literature. His point was that *Bhagavad-gītā* clearly advises us not to try to correct our environment, but to correct ourselves, to adjust with the environment. That is the key to the advice of *Bhagavad-gītā*: "Cure thyself." We have no power to bring about changes in the environment. That is arranged by the divine will. Our environment, the sum total of all the forces acting outside us, is irremovable. We have no ability to interfere with our environment; that will only be a useless loss of energy. Rather, we must try to correct ourselves so that we can adjust with the circumstances outside us: this is the key to our success in life *(tat te 'nukampāṁ susamīkṣamāṇo)*. We have our duty to perform, but we must not aspire after the results of our activities; the results depend on Krishna *(karmaṇy evādhikāras te mā phaleṣu kadācana)*. We make our contribution; at the same time, thousands of millions of others are contributing, creating the environment. So, we must do our duty, but we will have to accept the ultimate result as best, because it is arranged by the Absolute. There are so many results to our individual activities, but we must see how the absolute will harmonize everything and adjust ourselves accordingly.

Our responsibility lies only in discharging our duty. We must never aspire after any definite environment; the environment will go on in its own way. We have no power to change it. Rather, we must try our best to change our own self so that we may come in harmony with the environment.

*Bhagavad-gītā*—the highest spiritual literature. The Supreme Lord Krishna instructs Arjuna, "Cure thyself."

Our responsibility is never in enjoying the results of our actions. Because we work for a particular result and don't obtain it, should we be discouraged? No. We should go on doing our own duty. Whatever we contribute should be offered to the infinite, and the infinite will mold the results in His own way. Krishna says, "Never aspire after any particular result for your action. At the same time, don't be idle. Don't be worthless. Go on discharging your duty without depending on any outside consequence."

**Student:** Will we have to remember Krishna while we are doing this?

**Śrīdhar Mahārāj:** Yes. Then we will be able to come in connection with Krishna and gradually we will come to realize that our environment is friendly to us. When the reactions of our previous actions disappear, we will find that every wave is carrying good news to us. When our egoistic attitude vanishes, we will find ourself in the midst of sweet waves all around. We should try to do away with whatever wrong we have done hitherto. We must do our duty and never expect any definite result, but cast it towards the infinite.

## DISSOLVING EGO

And then one day will come when our egoistic feeling will dissolve and from within, our real self, a member of the infinite world, will spring up and awaken, and we will find ourselves in the sweet waves of that environment. There, everything is sweet. The breeze is sweet, the water is sweet, the trees are sweet, whatever we come in contact with is sweet, sweet, sweet.

Our internal ego is our enemy, and to dissolve that ego, we must do our duty as we think fit, but never expect any response according to our will. If we adopt this *karma-yoga* then in no time we will find that the wrong ego, which was always expecting something crooked for its selfish purpose, has vanished; the broad, wide ego within has come out, and we are in harmony with the whole universe. The harmonious world will appear before us, and the cover of selfish desires will disappear.

The cause of our disease is not outside us, but within us. A *paramahaṁsa* Vaiṣṇava, a saint of the highest platform, sees that everything is all right. He finds nothing to complain about. When one can see that everything is good and sweet to the furthest extreme, he comes to live in the plane of divinity. Our false ego creates only disturbance, and that ego should be dissolved. We should not think that the environment is our enemy. We must try hard to detect God's grace in whatever comes to us, even if it comes as an apparent enemy. Everything is the grace of the Lord, but we can't see it; rather, we see the opposite. The dirt is in our eyes.

Actually, everything is divine. It is all the grace of the Lord. The disease is in our eyes. We are diseased, and if the disease is cured, we shall find that we are in the midst of a gracious world. Only the coverings of desire deceive us from having a real estimation of the world. A bonafide student of the devotional school will accept such an attitude towards the environment and towards the Lord. We have to think that God's will is everywhere. Even a blade of grass cannot move without the sanction of the Supreme Authority. Every detail is detected and controlled by Him. We have to look upon the environment with optimism. The pessimism is within us. Our ego is responsible for all sorts of evil.

## INFINITE BLISSFULNESS

This is Vaiṣṇavism. If we can do this, then in no time, our disease will be cured, and we'll be in the midst of infinite blissfulness. Our tendency at present is to cure what we see on the outside. We think, "I want everything to follow my control, my sweet will. When everything obeys me, then I will be happy." But we must take just the opposite attitude. As Mahāprabhu has said:

**tṛṇād api sunīcena**
**taror api sahiṣṇunā**
**amāninā mānadena**
**kīrtanīyaḥ sadā hariḥ**

We should create no resistance against our environment. Still, if some undesirable things come towards us, we should tolerate that with our utmost patience. And even if someone attacks us we won't become violent; we must practice forbearance to the extreme. We shall honor everyone; we will seek no honor.

In this way, with the least amount of energy and time we can attain the highest goal: the plane where Krishna Himself is living. That is the most fundamental plane of existence. At that time, all the encasements covering the soul will vanish and die, and the inner soul will awaken and find that he is playing in a sweet wave, dancing and merry-making in Vṛndāvana, with Krishna and His devotees. And what is Vṛndāvana? It is neither a fable, nor a concocted story. The broadest and widest plane of the whole universe is beauty, sweetness, and blissfulness, and that is present in Vṛndāvana in all its fullness. We have to dive deep into that plane of reality.

Our ego has floated us on the surface of trouble in *māyā*, illusion. Concoction, and the search for selfish satisfaction have taken us here, and these must be dissolved once and for all. And then from within, our golden selves will come out, and we will find that we are in the plane of a happy dancing mood, with Krishna in Vṛndāvana.

## HEGEL'S "SELF-DETERMINATION"

In Hegelian language, this is called "self-determination." Self-determination means we must die to live. We must leave our material life and all our material habits; we have to die as we are if we want to have a real life. We must give up our false ego. Our material habits from different births are collected in the ego in subtle forms, not only from the experience of human birth, but even from animal births, tree births, and so many other births. Krishna consciousness means the wholesale dissolution of the false ego. That concocted, selfish figure within us is our enemy. The real self is hopelessly buried beneath the false ego. So great is the depth of our forgetfulness that we do not even know who we are. So, as the German philosopher Hegel said, we have to "die to live."

Reality is for itself and by itself. The world is not created for our selfish end; it has a universal end, and we are part and parcel of that. We must come to an understanding with the whole. The complete whole is Krishna and he is dancing, playing, and singing in His own way. We must enter into that harmonious dance.

Being infinitesimal, should we think that the infinite must be controlled by us? That by our whim everything will go on? This is the most crooked, heinous object ever conceived, and we are suffering from such a disease. This is the real problem in society. Our inquiry should be aimed at solving this.

**Student:** Does this mean we have to give up material life completely?

**Śrīdhar Mahārāj:** Not at once. Everyone must progress gradually, according to his own particular case. If one who has much affinity towards worldly life suddenly leaves that, he may not keep up his vows; he may go down again. So, according to personal capacity we must make gradual progress. That is to be taken into consideration, but still, we should always be eager to give up everything and devote ourselves exclusively to the highest duty. Those who have enough courage will jump into the unknown, thinking, "Krishna will protect me. I am jumping in the name of God. He is everywhere; He will take me on His lap." With this idea, one who has real eagerness for the truth may leap forward.

**Student:** I have a problem. For ten years I've tried to take up this process. For ten years, I have kept from eating meat, fish, and eggs. I avoid material things—I have no attraction for them. I have left all this behind. But there is one thing I want to give up and also I don't want to give up. This is *gañja* (marijuana).

**Śrīdhar Mahārāj:** That is a small thing. There are three real difficulties: the first is women, the second is money, and the third, good name and fame. These three are our enemies. Marijuana intoxication is a small thing. Anyone can give it up easily. But these three things are the fundamental aspiration of every animal, tree, bird, man, or god. These three are everywhere. But intoxication and other fleeting habits are very negligible things and can be conquered very easily.

As we have gradually come into the habit of intoxication, we have to come out; gradually, and not suddenly. Just after World War Two, we read in the newspaper that Goering, Hitler's air general, was habituated to taking much intoxication. But when he was put into jail, no intoxication was supplied to him. He became sick, but treatment went on and he was cured. His disease was cured by the medicine. We also have seen so many opium-eaters who came here, joined the temple, and gradually left their habit.

Many so-called *sādhus* smoke marijuana. It helps concentration, but that is the material mind. It disturbs faith. It is an enemy to faith. No material intoxication, but only faith can take us to our desired goal. The misguided souls think that marijuana, hashish, and so many other things can help us in our meditation. It may do something, but that is mundane and that will frustrate us in our time of need. These things cannot help us rise up very high.

## SEX, DOPE, AND GOLD

*Śrīmad-Bhāgavatam* (1.17.38) advises that these five things should be rejected: *dyūtaṁ*: gambling, or diplomacy; *pānaṁ*: intoxication, including tea, coffee, betel, and everything else; *striyaḥ*: unlawful, illegal womanlove; *sūnā*: butchering; and the transaction of gold. Trade in gold makes one very apathetic towards progress in the line of faith. These five are very tempting.

What to speak of the mania that intoxication will help us in our meditation upon the transcendental, Devarṣi Nārada says, *yamādibhir yoga-pathaiḥ kāma-lobha-hato muhuḥ*: even what we acquire by meditation is temporary and has no permanent effect. Only real faith in the line of pure devotion can help us.

## SAINTS: LIVING SCRIPTURES

**Student:** So, how can we develop our faith in Krishna consciousness?

**Śrīdhar Mahārāj:** How have you come to conceive of Krishna consciousness?

**Student:** By reading *Bhagavad-gītā*.

**Śrīdhar Mahārāj:** *Bhagavad-gītā*. From the scriptures. And the scriptures are written by whom? Some saint. So, the association of saints and the advice of scriptures are both necessary. The saint is the living scripture, and the scripture advises us in a passive way. A saint can actively approach us, and passively we may receive benefit from the scriptures. The association of the scriptures and the saints can help us achieve the ultimate realization: *sādhu śāstra kṛpaya haya*. The saints are more powerful. Those who are living the life of the scriptural advice are scripture personified. In their association, and by their grace, we can imbibe such higher, subtle knowledge and faith.

All our experiences are futile in the attempt to attain the ultimate destination; only faith can lead us there. The spiritual world is far, far beyond the jurisdiction of our limited visual, aural, and mental experience. The experience of the eye, ear, and mind is very meager and limited, but faith can rise up and pierce through this area, and enter the transcendental realm.

Faith should be developed with the help of scriptures and saints. They will help us understand that the spiritual world is real and this world is unreal. At that time, this material world will be night to us, and that will be day. Presently, the eternal world is darkness to us, and we are awake in this mortal world. What is night to one is day to another. A saint is awake in some matter, and a *dacoit* (thief) is working in another plane. They are living in two separate worlds. A scientist is living in one world; a rowdy is living in another. One's day is night to another. The ordinary persons cannot see what Einstein and Newton have seen, and what the ordinary man sees is ignored by a great man. So, we have to awaken our interest in that plane, and ignore the interests of this plane.

Śrīla Śrīdhar Mahārāj lecturing at his *āśrama* in Nabadwīp, India. "The association of scriptures and saints can help us achieve the ultimate realization."

## WORLD WAR III: LET IT BE

**Student:** Many people are worried about nuclear war. They think it may come very soon.

**Śrīdhar Mahārāj:** That is a point on a line, a line on a plane, a plane in a solid. So many times wars are coming and going; so many times the sun, the Earth, and the solar systems disappear, and again spring up. We are in the midst of such thought in eternity. This nuclear war is a tiny point; what of that? Individuals are dying at every moment; the Earth will die, the whole human section will disappear. Let it be.

We must try to live in eternity; not any particular span of time or space. We must prepare ourselves for our eternal benefit, not for any temporary remedy. The sun, the moon, and all the planets appear and vanish: they die, and then again, they are created. Within such an eternity we have to live. Religion covers that aspect of our existence. We are told to view things from this standpoint: not only this body, but the human race, the animals, the trees, the entire Earth, and even the sun, will all vanish, and again spring up. Creation, dissolution, creation, dissolution—it will continue forever in the domain of misconception. At the same time, there is another world which is eternal; we are requested to enter there, to make our home in that plane which neither enters into the jaws of death, nor suffers any change.

In the *Bhagavad-gītā (8.16)* it is stated:

**ābrahma-bhuvanāl lokāḥ**
**punar āvartino 'rjuna**
**mām upetya tu kaunteya**
**punar janma na vidyate**

"Even Lord Brahmā, the creator himself, has to die. Up to Brahmāloka, the highest planet in the material world, the whole material energy undergoes such changes."

But if we can cross the area of misunderstanding and enter the area of proper understanding, then there is no creation or dissolution. That is eternal, and we are children of that soil. Our bodies and minds are children of this soil which comes and goes, which is created and then dies. We have to get out of this world of death.

## ZONE OF NECTAR

We are in such an area. What is to be done? Try to get out. Try your best to get out of this mortal area. The saints inform us, "Come home dear friend, let us go home. Why are you suffering so much trouble unnecessarily in a foreign land? The spiritual world is real; this material world is unreal: springing and vanishing, coming and going, it is a farce! From the world of farce we must come to reality. Here in this material world there will be not only one war, but wars after wars, wars after wars.

There is a zone of nectar, and we are actually children of that nectar that does not die (*śṛṇvantu viśve amṛtasya putrāḥ*). Somehow, we are misguided here, but really we are children of that soil which is eternal, where there is no birth or death. With a wide and broad heart, we have to approach there. This is declared by Śrī Chaitanya Mahāprabhu, and the *Bhagavad-gītā*, the *Upaniṣads*, and the *Śrīmad-Bhāgavatam* all confirm the same thing. That is our very sweet, sweet home, and we must try our best to go back to God, back to home, and take others with us.

# Fossilism vs. Subjective Evolution

*The following chapter is an excerpt from a conversation between* Śrīla Śrīdhar *Mahārāj and neurophysiologist Dr. Daniel Murphey, Ph.D.*

Darwin has given the theory of evolution—Fossilism. *Vedānta* has given subjective evolution. In Darwin's theory of objective evolution, matter evolves consciousness. The object exists first, and by its development, life is coming, consciousness is coming—from stone. That is objective evolution. But an object is a relative term; without the subject, an object cannot stand. The subject is the primary substance. Whatever is to be felt is only an idea in the subjective ocean. So, the subject, consciousness is first. The object, the gross, proceeds from the subtle.

When a particular potency is handled by Krishna, in His form as Maha-Viṣṇu, then the material energy begins to move and produce something *(mayādhyakṣeṇa prakṛtiḥ sūyate sa-carācaram)*. The first product is a general ego. Then, gradually so many plural individual egos emanate from the general ego. The experience of this world develops from ego. When ego contacts the mode of ignorance, form is produced. When it contacts the mode of goodness, the sun and light are produced. When false ego comes in connection with these three modes of nature, a division takes place, and the objects of the senses, the material senses, and the power of sense perception are generated. So, from the subtle, the gross is coming.

## THE GHOST OF DARWIN

That is Vedāntic evolution. But the Darwin theory says that from the gross, the subtle is coming. At present, people are fond of the Darwin theory that stone produces consciousness. Darwin's objective evolution has swallowed us. Although externally, we reject it, we hate it, still, the ghost of Darwin's theory has devoured everyone. Therefore, it is difficult to make them understand that consciousness is more valuable than stone. It's easy for consciousness to produce stone; it is difficult for stone to produce consciousness. Consciousness is more valuable; stone is less valuable. So, a more valuable thing can produce a less valuable thing, but it is difficult to explain how a less valuable thing can produce something more valuable.

## FOSSIL FATHERS

The material scientists think that the subtle proceeds from the gross. This is upside-down. It is just the opposite. Not "fossil-fatherism," but "God-fatherism." Their theory is "fossil-fatherism": the fossil is the father of everyone. The scientists believe that everything moves upward. This is incorrect. It is coming down. This is described in the *Bhagavad-gītā* (15.1):

**ūrdhva-mūlam adhaḥ-śākham**
**aśvatthaṁ prāhur avyayam**
**chandāṁsi yasya parṇāni**
**yas taṁ veda sa veda-vit**

"The tree of this material world has its roots upward, while its branches extend downward. The leaves of this tree are the Vedic hymns. One who understands this tree, and its origin, is a true knower of the *Vedas*." So, according to Vedic knowledge, everything moves from up to down, not from down to up.

Matter does not produce the soul; rather the soul contains in its one negligible portion the conception of matter. Like an eczema, it is a disease. The world exists like an eczema in a wholesome body. This is the Vedāntic understanding. It would certainly be a wonderful miracle if stone could produce the soul, but it is easier and more reasonable for us to think that the soul has produced the conception of stone. In the soul, there are many conceptions, and one conception is that of stone. It is all in the plane of consciousness. But that stone can produce soul, or consciousness, is difficult, ridiculous, inconceivable, and unreasonable. Rather, it is the opposite, something like the Berkeley theory that the world is in the mind, and not that the mind is in the world. It is only our deviation from the truth that brings us into this mundane world. How and where that deviation begins is to be thought out. But deviation from the truth has brought us to this false area.

So, consciousness is producing everything. Consciousness is eternal; this world is not eternal. This is a temporary production, and the temporary stone cannot produce eternal consciousness. Pure consciousness is an eternal subject *(nitya sanātana)*. It is not a product; it is *productive*. Ether can produce fire, and earth, but the earth cannot produce ether. The subtle is more efficient than the gross. The gross is of secondary importance. The soul, *ātmā*, is of principle importance. The origin of everything must be conscious; the starting point must begin with the interested party. The soul is endowed with interest, but a stone has no interest, plan, or project, nothing of the kind. But there is a plan and a purpose pervading everything, and that is the important thing. According to that consideration, the characteristic of the Absolute, the original substance should be calculated. An object of limited attributes and capacity cannot be the ultimate cause. Only a thing of unlimited quality and capacity should be taken as the cause of the whole. That is a more reasonable idea. Science should realize this. So, there are some who think that science is gradually trying to meet philosophy.

## KARMIC BOOMERANG

Material science is only increasing the circumference of the mortal world. But increasing the tendency of exploitation cannot help us. Science is only borrowing, extorting power from nature. According to Newton: "For every action there is an equal and opposite reaction." We must be conscious of this fact. All our acquisition here is nothing: like a boomerang, it will come back to zero again. So scientific progress is no progress. It is "progress" in the wrong direction. Actually, the first principle of any living body is to save himself. That is the first principle, and that should be our starting point.

In the *Upaniṣads* it is said:

**asato mā sad gamāya**
**tāmaso mā jyotir gamāya**
**mṛtyor mā amṛtaṁ gamāya**

"I am mortal; make me eternal. I am ignorant, filled with nescience; take me to science, knowledge. And I am threatened with misery; guide me towards bliss". We should begin our research work in these three phases: how to save one's own self and save the world; how to remove darkness and attain light; and how to remove misery and taste nectar, the sweet life of eternity, knowledge, and bliss *(sac-cid-ānandam, satyam śivam sundaram)*.

## SCIENCE DEVOURS ITSELF

This should be the line of our search; all other inquiries are false. This so-called scientific research is a wild goose chase. It is suicidal. The atomic researchers will soon prove that this kind of science devours itself; it sucks its own blood. It will live, feeding on its own flesh and the flesh of its friends. Material scientific knowledge is no knowledge. We must acquaint ourselves with a vital understanding of pure, real knowledge. We must absorb ourselves and others in that knowledge, remove darkness and bring light, remove misery and establish eternal peace.

Science means *not* to extend the jurisdiction of exploitation, knowing full well there will be a reaction. By extending the space of exploitation, we will also surely be exploited. If one knowingly commits an offense, then he is charged with more punishment. So, so-called scientific advancement is suicidal. And it is clearly proven: presently the leading countries of the world are threatening each other with atomic weapons, the highest product of the scientists.

## NEUTRON BOMB: DEATH RAY

What is the difference between the atomic bomb and the neutron bomb? The neutron bomb is something like a death-ray that will kill the people, but will not destroy the buildings. The neutron bomb: man will be killed, the houses, the buildings and everything else will be left behind. The bed will be there, the furniture, everything else will be there, but only the life will be gone, and the bodies will become rotten. That is the effect of the neutron bomb.

And those who emerge victorious will come to enjoy all these things. They will have to remove the dead bodies, and fill the place up with their own men. This is action and reaction in the plane of exploitation.

So, this is a suicidal civilization. The whole civilization is rotten to the bottom. They are exploiting nature for the apparent good of human society, but it is incurring a loan from nature that must be paid to the farthing with interest. Because they do not believe this, they will have no relief. They will be forced to clear the debt; nature won't forgive them. Nature is there like a computer, calculating. So, this civilization is anti-civilization. The whole thing is rotten, a camouflage, a treachery to the soul-world. But our policy is different; plain living and high thinking.

Our policy should be to make the best use of a bad bargain. Somehow or other, we have already come here, so now we have to utilize our time and energy in such a way that with the least exploitation we can get out of this world.

*—Editor's note: shortly after this meeting, Dr. Murphey became an initiated disciple of Śrīla Śrīdhar Mahārāj.*

# Origin Of The Soul

*Since time immemorial, man has inquired about the origin of the soul. In this brief chapter, Śrīla Śrīdhar Mahārāj answers this most vital of all questions: "Who am I? Where have I come from?"*

How does the soul first appear in this world? From what stage of spiritual existence does he fall into the material world? This is a broad question, which requires some background information.

There are two classes of souls, *jīvas*, who come into this world. One class comes from the spiritual Vaikuṇṭha planets by the necessity of *nitya-līlā*, the eternal pastimes of Krishna. Another comes by constitutional necessity.

The *brahmajyoti*, the nondifferentiated marginal plane, is the source of infinite *jīva souls*, atomic spiritual particles of nondifferentiated character. The rays of the Lord's transcendental body are known as the *brahmajyoti*, and a pencil of a ray of the *brahmajyoti is* the *jīva*. The *jīva* soul is an atom in that effulgence, and the *brahmajyoti* is a product of an infinite number of *jīva* atoms.

Generally, souls emanate from the *brahmajyoti* which is living and growing. Within the *brahmajyoti*, their equilibrium is somehow disturbed and movement begins. From nondifferentiation, differentiation begins. From a plain sheet of uniform consciousness, individual conscious units grow. And because the *jīva* is conscious, it is endowed with free will. So, from the marginal position they choose either the side of exploitation or the side of dedication.

*Kṛṣṇa bhuli' sei jīva anādi bahirmukha. Anādi* means that which has no beginning. When we enter the land of exploitation, we come within the factor of time, space, and thought. And when we come to exploit, action and reaction begins in the negative land of loan. Although we strive to become masters, really we become losers.

Goloka and Vaikuṇṭha servitors are also seen to be within the jurisdiction of the *brahmaṇḍa*, the material universe, but that is only a play, *līlā*. They come from that higher plane only to take part in the Lord's pastimes and then return. The fallen souls come from the marginal position within the *brahmajyoti*, and not from Vaikuṇṭha.

The first position of a soul in the material world will be like that of Brahmā, the creator. Then his *karma* may take him to the body of a beast like a tiger, where he is surrounded with a tigerish mentality, or to the body of a tree or creeper, where different impressions may surround him. In this way, one is involved in action and reaction. The case is complex; to analyze the details of the history of a particular atom is unnecessary. We are concerned with the general thing: how the transformation of the material conception springs from pure consciousness.

## ELECTRONS OF CONSCIOUSNESS

Matter is not independent of spirit. In the *brahma-jyoti* we are equipoised in the marginal potency as an infinite number of pinpoints of spiritual rays, electrons of consciousness. Consciousness means endowed with free will, for without free will no consciousness can be conceived. An atomic pinpoint of consciousness has very meager free will, and by misuse of their free will some *jīvas* have taken their chance in the material world. They refused to submit to the supreme authority; they wanted to dominate. So, with this germinal idea of domination, the *jīva* enters into the world of exploitation. In the *Bhagavad-gītā* (7.27) it is stated:

**icchā-dveṣa samutthena**
**dvandva-mohena bhārata**
**sarva-bhūtāni sammohaṁ**
**sarge yānti parantapa**

"Two principles in a crude form awaken in the *jīva*: hatred and desire. Then, gradually the soul comes down to mingle with the mundane world." At first, sympathy and apathy develop in a crude form, just as when a sprout springs up with two leaves. And gradually these two things help us to dive deep into this mundane world.

Upon retiring from the world of exploitation, the soul may return to his former position in the *brahmajyoti* as spirit. But, if the soul has gathered the tendency of dedication through his previous devotional activities, he does not stop there; he pierces through the *brahmajyoti* and goes towards Vaikuṇṭha.

Why has the soul come to the world of exploitation, and not the world of dedication? That should be attributed to his innate nature, which is endowed with free will. It is a free choice. This is substantiated in the *Bhagavad-gītā* (5. 14):

**na kartṛtvaṁ na karmāṇi**
**lokasya sṛjati prabhuḥ**
**na karma-phala-saṁyogaṁ**
**svabhāvas tu pravartate**

"The soul is responsible for his entrance into the land of exploitation." The responsibility is with the soul; otherwise, the Lord would be responsible for his distressed condition. But Krishna says that the soul's innate freewill is responsible for his entanglement in the material world. The soul is conscious, and consciousness means endowed with freedom. Because the soul is atomic, his freewill is imperfect and vulnerable. The result of that free choice is that some are coming into the material world, and some are going to the spiritual world. So, the responsibility is with the individual soul.

## THE RIGHT TO WRONG

Once, an Indian political leader, Śyāmasundar Chakravartī, asked our spiritual master, Prabhupād, "Why has the Lord granted such freedom to the *jīva*?" Prabhupād told him, "You are fighting for freedom. Don't you know the value of freedom? Devoid of freedom, the soul is only matter." Freedom offers us the alternative to do right or wrong. Once, Gandhi told the British authorities, "We want freedom." They replied, "You are not fit to have self-government. When you are fit, we shall give it to you." But finally, he told them, "We want the freedom to do wrong." So, freedom does not guarantee only acting in the right way; freedom has its value independent of right and wrong.

Freewill is only absolute with the Absolute Truth. Because we are finite, our freewill is infinitesimal. The possibility of committing a mistake is there. Our first choice was to dominate, and so, gradually we have entered the world of domination. As a result of this first action, everything else has developed. So, in different ranks, the species have been divided, from the demigods down to the trees and stones. And watery bodies, gaseous bodies, anything that we find here has evolved in that way. The activating principle in any form of embryological development is the soul, and from the soul, everything has evolved.

# Knowledge Above Mortality

Knowledge above mortality is knowledge proper. Mundane knowledge has no value, for it does not endure. We must inquire elsewhere for permanent knowledge. Real knowledge is stable; it has a firm foundation, and Vedic education deals with how to acquire that knowledge. The meaning of the word *veda* is "Know." No rhyme or reason is shown why you should know, and no explanation is given: simply "Know."

Because doubt is absent in the spiritual plane, no cheating is possible. It is a simple, direct transaction—"Know." In that transcendental plane, everyone is a confidential friend, and they are stainless in their conduct. No cheating tendency is possible there, so there is no suspicion. Here, we are in the plane of misunderstanding and doubt, so we want to examine everything. We are living in a vulnerable and vitiated plane, where people cheat one another. We cannot rely on others, for they may deceive us. But where cheating is unknown, transactions are very simple and straightforward. So, no reason is given for suggestions that come down from that plane. Now, the question arises how to attain that sort of true, comprehensive, and non-deceptive knowledge? In the *Bhagavad-gītā* (4.34) Krishna says:

**tad viddhi praṇipātena**
**paripraśnena sevayā**
**upadekṣyanti te jñānaṁ**
**jñāninas tattva-darśinaḥ**

"To learn knowledge above mortality you must approach a self-realized soul, accept him as your spiritual master and take initiation from him. Inquire submissively, and render service unto him. Self-realized souls can impart knowledge unto you, for they have seen the truth."

### SUPERKNOWLEDGE

We have to approach the domain of knowledge with self-surrender, honest inquiry, and a serving attitude. We have to approach that plane with the mentality of slavery. Higher knowledge will not serve a person of lower status. If we want perfect knowledge at all, we will have to serve the Supreme Lord. He will use us for His own purpose; not that we will use Him. We may be subjects in this mundane world, but we will have to become objects to be handled by the superknowledge of that plane. If we want to connect with that higher knowledge, we must approach with this attitude.

*Praṇipāta* means that I have finished my experience here; I have no charm or aspiration for anything in this world. Then there is *paripraśna*, or honest, submissive, and humble inquiry with sincere eagerness, and not with a challenging mood; otherwise perfect knowledge won't care to descend to us. Krishna is already full in Himself, so we have to enter His domain only to fulfill His purpose. He can't be subservient to us, for we are tiny persons with meager experience and a conception of mean fulfillment. We cannot handle Him; we can approach Him only if we like to be handled by Him. So, such a favorable environment should be created where real knowledge is to be cultivated. That knowledge is supreme, and cannot be subservient to the mundane conception, the world of mortality. It is *sac-cid-ānanda*. *Sat* means unassailable existence, *cit* means consciousness, and *ānanda* means beauty and pleasure.

"I must try to relieve myself of my present material miseries and inquire after a proper land where I can live happily." Having come to this conclusion, we will have to search for a person who is a bonafide agent of the higher world and consult with him about how we can be relieved from this present undesirable environment. In the *Śrīmad-Bhāgavatam* (11.3.21) it is said:

**tasmād guruṁ prapadyeta**
**jijñāsuḥ śreyaḥ uttamam**
**śābde pare ca niṣṇātaṁ**
**brahmaṇy upaśamāśrayam**

"What is the conception of real good, and who is considered to be a bonafide agent of the truth? One who has knowledge of the scripture that has descended from the upper domain, who has theoretical as well as practical knowledge of higher truth, must be approached by a bonafide inquirer, for such a qualified spiritual master can impart proper knowledge to the sincere student." In the *Muṇḍaka Upaniṣad* (1.2.12) it is also stated:

**tad-vijñānārthaṁ sa gurum evābhigacchet**
**samit-pāṇiḥ śrotriyaṁ brahma-niṣṭham**

"In order to learn transcendental knowledge, one must approach a genuine spiritual master coming in disciplic succession, who is fixed in the Absolute Truth."

In this verse, the word *tata* means "after this." When one's calculation is finished, he thinks, "Life is not worth living here in this world of birth, death, old age, and disease. I must have a better world in which to live, where I can live as a gentleman. At every moment death is devouring everything. Birth, death, old age, and disease — all these troubles prevent me from fulfilling my ambitions here. I want something categorically different." At that time, taking the responsibility on his own shoulders, without giving any trouble to the *guru*, and at the risk of poverty, ill-feeding, and so many other hardships, he will approach the *guru*. It is a free transaction. Not that he will give something to *gurudeva*, but he will collect what is necessary for sacrifice, for education, and at his own risk he will approach the spiritual master.

## Knowledge Through Sound

And what will be the position of the *guru*? He will be well-versed in the scriptures, the *śruti-śāstra*, or that knowledge which can only be acquired through the medium of sound, by attentive earnest hearing (*śrotriyaṁ brahma-niṣṭham*).

*Brahmā niṣṭham* means, "One who is established in *brahman*, spirit, and who is acquainted with the causal position of the universe." That is described in the *Upanisads*:

**yeto vā imāni bhūtāni jāyante,**
**yena jātāni jīvanti**
**yat prayanty abhisaṁviśanti**
**tad vijijñāsasva**
**tad eva brahma**

—*Taittirīya Upaniṣad* 3.1

"The Supreme Brahman is the origin and shelter of all living beings. When there is a creation, He brings them forth from their original state, and at the time of annihilation, He devours them. After creation, everything rests in His omnipotence, and after annihilation, everything again returns to rest in Him." These are the confirmations of the Vedic hymns.

**yasmin vijñāte sarvam evaṁ vijñātaṁ bhavati**
**yasmin prāpte sarvam idaṁ prāptam bhavati**

"By knowing Him, everything is known; by getting Him, everything is gained." We have come to inquire about *Brahman*, the biggest, the all-accommodating principle by knowing which we can know anything and everything. And it is possible; it is not impossible. The *Upaniṣads* say, "If you want to know anything, then know the whole. And what is the nature of the whole? Everything is coming from Him, everything is being maintained by Him, and again everything enters into Him. That is *Brahman*; so try to know that. If you can know that, everything will be known to you."

This is also explained in the *Śrīmad-Bhāgavatam* (4.31.14):

**yathā taror mūla-niṣecanena**
**tṛpyanti tat-skandha-bhujopaśākhāḥ**
**prāṇopahārāc ca yathendriyāṇāṁ**
**tathaiva sarvārhaṇam acyutejyā**

"Just as if you pour water onto the root of a tree, the whole tree is fed, and just as when you supply food to the stomach, the whole body is fed, so if you can gain knowledge of the prime cause, *Brahman*, then you can know anything and everything." Faith in this is called *śraddhā*.

The *Vedānta-sūtra*, the very gist of the *Vedas*, says *athāto brahmā jijñāsa*: "Now that you have finished with the fruitive activities recommended in the *karma-kāṇḍa* section of the *Vedas* by Jaimini, we ask you to inquire about Brahman."

That is described in the *Śrīmad-Bhāgavatam* (1.1.1) *janmādy asya yato 'nvayād itarataś cārtheṣv abhijñaḥ svarāt*: "Friends, let us inquire into the prime cause, whose nature is such that whatever we can see, and whatever we can conceive of, springs from Him. He is the ultimate cause of everything, both directly and indirectly."

Only He knows the purpose for which all things are created and maintained. Only He knows where all things will go. Only He is aware of that fact —no one else.

*Artheṣv abhijñaḥ svarāt*, means that He knows the meaning of every incident in existence and that He is above giving any explanation to others. He is not responsible to any law or to anyone else. He is absolute and independent.

## VEDIC REVELATION

And how do we know that? He has extended knowledge of Himself through the *Vedas*. *Brahma* means *Veda*. So, by the line of inspiration, or revelation, Vedic knowledge was transmitted to the first living being, the creator of the world, Lord Brahmā (*tene bṛahma hṛdā ya ādi kavaye*). The scholars of the world fail to understand the strategy and nature of that sort of knowledge. They cannot follow the vital and fundamental points of Vedic knowledge, such as the transformation of one thing into another (*muhyanti yat sūrayaḥ*). Water may be transformed into gas, gas may be transformed into ether, earth may be transformed into heat: by such a process, we can understand the existence of this world (*tejo vāri mṛdāṁ yathā vinimayo yatra tri-sargo 'mṛṣā*), for by the transformation of the Lord's energy, this world comes into being. This transformation involves the three mode of nature; *tamas*, *rajas*, and *sattva*. *Tama* means hard, static matter. *Raja*

अथ श्रीमद्भगवद्गीता

अथ प्रथमोऽध्यायः

धृतराष्ट्र उवाच

धर्मक्षेत्रे कुरुक्षेत्रे समवेता युयुत्सवः ।
मामकाः पाण्डवाश्चैव किमकुर्वत संजय ॥

संजय उवाच

दृष्ट्वा तु पाण्डवानीकं व्यूढं दुर्योधनस्तदा ।
आचार्यमुपसङ्गम्य राजा वचनमब्रवीत् ॥
पश्यैतां पाण्डुपुत्राणामाचार्य महतीं चमूम् ।
व्यूढां द्रुपदपुत्रेण तव शिष्येण धीमता ॥

The original Sanskrit text of the *Bhagavad-gitā*, the essence of all Vedic knowledge, recorded more than fifty centuries ago in the Himalayas by the sage Vyāsa.

means energy, and *sattva* means spirit, light, knowledge. So, by transformation this world has been created.

In His abode, which is illumined by the ray of His own knowledge, there is no possibility of deception or misunderstanding. (*dhāmnā svena sadā nirasta-kuhakaṁ satyaṁ paraṁ dhīmahi*).

Here, we are being deceived through misunderstanding. We have entered a plane of existence where the whole world is full of misconception, falsity, and miscalculation. We are presently living in the world of *māyā*. *Māyā* means *mā-yā*: "What is not." I am seeing something which is really something else.

## REALITY: BY ITSELF AND FOR ITSELF

*Īśāvāsyam* —everything is meant for God. That is the Hegelian theory: reality is by itself and for itself. Hegel is the founder of Ideal Realism, so he says, "Reality is by itself and for itself." "By itself," means that He is His own cause; no one has created Him. Otherwise, whoever had created Him would have primary importance. "For itself," means that God exists only to fulfill His own purpose. This is the universal truth: everything is for Him, and nothing is for anyone else. So, when we think that the things around us are meant for us, or for our nation, or for the human beings, this is all a false calculation, and knowledge based on such a miscalculation has its reaction.

"To every action, there is an equal and opposite reaction." I am eating something; it is entitled to eat me. In the *Manu Saṁhitā*, the word *māṁsaḥ* is used to indicate meat. *Māṁ* means "Me," *saḥ* means "he." *Māṁsaḥ* means "me-he." What is the meaning? I am eating him; and he will eat me afterwards as a reaction. He is entitled to devour me, as I am at present devouring him. This is the underlying meaning—every action, whatever it is, has its reaction. This is confirmed in the *Bhagavad-gītā* (3.9):

**yajñārthāt karmaṇo 'nyatra**
**loko 'yaṁ karma-bandhanaḥ**
**tad-arthaṁ karma kaunteya**
**mukta-saṅgaḥ samācara**

"Unless work is done as a sacrifice for Viṣṇu, one's own work will be the cause of bondage; therefore work on My behalf, and free yourself from the chain of action and reaction." *Bhagavad-gītā* says that any work, no matter what it is, causes a reaction. For example, you may nurse a patient. Apparently, it is a good thing, but you are giving the patient medicine that comes from killing so many insects, trees, creepers, and animals. You may think that your nursing is a very pure duty, but you are causing a disturbance in the environment, and you will have to pay for that. In this way, whatever we do here cannot be perfectly good. The German philosopher Kant has said, "Without good will, no action can be perfectly good." But we are of the opinion that even good will is impossible here in this mundane plane. According to Kant, good will is a pure thing, whereas no action here can be perfect, but we say that even good will is impossible in the relative calculation of the world, because we are plodding in the mud of misunderstanding.

Pure knowledge comes only from above, and we

have to learn to accept that. When that sort of understanding comes within us, it is known as *śraddhā*, or faith. Faith is also a great thing. We should have faith that if we do our duty towards the absolute, then all our duties to the environment in all directions are automatically done (*Kṛṣṇe bhakti kaile sarva karma kṛta haya*). By satisfying Krishna, the whole universe becomes satisfied, for one who is dear to Krishna is dear to the whole universe (*yasmin tuṣṭe jagat tuṣṭam prīṇite prīṇito jagat*). Just as by watering the root of the tree all the leaves and branches are automatically nourished, by fulfilling one's duty towards Lord Krishna all one's duties are automatically fulfilled.

## KRISHNA'S TRANSCENDENTAL ABODE

Everything is meant for Krishna. We are also meant for Him (*īśāvāsyaṁ idaṁ sarvaṁ*). This is true knowledge, and this is the true situation of the world. Exploitation is an incomplete and reactionary idea for which we incur a debt that we shall later have to pay. We may go to Satyaloka, the highest planet in the material universe, but by exploiting nature, we incur a debt, become heavy, and go down. And when we go down, others come to exploit and extort us until our debts are paid. Then the heaviness goes, and we become light and go upward to the higher planetary systems again. And when we go up, we exploit those who are in a lower position. In this way, there is continual exploitation and clearance of debt. This is confirmed in the *Bhagavad-gītā* (8.16):

**ā-brahma-bhuvanāl lokāḥ**
**punar āvartino 'rjuna**
**mām upetya tu kaunteya**
**punar janma na vidyate**

"All planetary systems within this world of matter are places of repeated birth and death, but one who attains My abode, O son of Kuntī, never takes birth again." Upon going there, one never returns to this material world *(yad gatvā na nivartante tad dhāma paramaṁ mama)*. Krishna's abode is *nirguṇa*, or transcendental to any material quality.

We must firmly establish the conception of *īśāvāsyaṁ*: everything, including ourselves, is meant for the Supreme Lord. We are all His servants, and we are meant to utilize everything in His service. Any work we perform will bind us in this environment of matter, unless we perform *yajña*, sacrifice *(yajñārthāt karmaṇo 'nyatra loko 'yaṁ karma-bandhanaḥ)*. And the *Vedas* enjoin, *yajño vai viṣṇu*: "Sacrifice is meant exclusively for Viṣṇu, or Krishna." This is confirmed in the *Bhagavad-gītā* (9.24), where Krishna says, "I am the only enjoyer of every sacrifice." *(ahaṁ hi sarva-yajñānāṁ bhoktā ca prabhur eva ca)*. Sacrifice is not meant for the country, or for the society, or for anything else. Sacrifice is meant only for the Supreme Lord. No one less than He is worthy of sacrifice. So, only by connecting our activities with the infinite can we be freed from the present environment of action and reaction.

When knowledge comes in connection with the absolute, it loses its filthy characteristic. Then we can have full knowledge, which will lead us to *prema-bhakti*, love of God. Everything is meant for Krishna. He is the only enjoyer of everything. He is the absolute autocrat, and He is the absolute good. We are all His servants, and everything is meant for His satisfaction. We must come to this understanding. The *guru-kula* system of Vedic education should be conceived in this line.

## GURU—HEAVIER THAN THE HIMALAYAS

*Guru* means "heavy." *Guru* means "one who dispels the darkness," and "who is heavy, who cannot be moved by any proposal." He is so well-established in the truth that no offer of alternative knowledge, or any other proposal, can move him from his position. He is firm there. He can help the *laghu*, the people who are very light; those whom anyone can handle like dolls of play. But the *guru* can never be moved from his position. He will sit tight there, heavier than the Himalayas, and face all fleeting conceptions of knowledge, breaking them right and left, and establishing the universal characteristic of absolute knowledge. He will impart knowledge of the Absolute Truth, *Brahman*, the supreme whole, dispelling all misconceptions and establishing knowledge of the absolute upon the throne of the heart. This is the conception of *guru-kula*, the Vedic system of education of ancient India.

The Vedic system of education deals with knowledge proper—not half-knowledge, but knowledge of the whole, which can deliver us from all troubles and guide us to the most desirable position. Nowadays, we can sell knowledge, but *this* knowledge cannot be sold. Intellectual knowledge can be taken into the market, but this knowledge cannot be taken into the market, for this is absolute knowledge. Vedic knowledge gives us our fulfillment of life, attaining which we will no longer feel the necessity to run here and there for any greater knowledge.

Previously, that knowledge was taught within the *guru-kula*, the ancient Vedic school. Vedic knowledge means knowledge which comes from outside the area of misunderstanding, miscalculation, and false historiography. The books recorded here are filled with temporary truths and misconceptions. Such things may be useful now, but after some time, it won't work; mundane law will have no position, and everything will be dissolved. The Earth will be dissolved. Matter will be dissolved, and we won't be able to trace any quality of matter when everything is reduced to ether. No trace of air, or heat, or anything else will remain in any way. With the dissolution of this mundane world, nothing will remain but transcendental knowledge.

## THE LAND OF DEDICATION

In the *Bhagavad-gītā* (15.6) Krishna says, "One who reaches My abode never returns to this material world (*yad gatvāna nivartante tad dhāma paramaṁ mama*). The dissolution will go on in the plane of the material world, but if you can secure a visa for that land, if you can enter into that soil, you will never be mishandled. When the sun, moon, and stars are all dissolved, your eternal self, your devotional ego, will be quite safe in My plane." The material world is the land of exploitation; the spiritual world is the opposite—the land of dedication. In the middle there is the *brahmajyoti*: the line of demarcation between exploitation and dedication.

Here in this material world, every unit is of an exploiting nature; there it is just the opposite. Everything there is wholly dedicated to the service of Krishna, and there is no want of anything, rather whatever is necessary to make service to Krishna possible comes automatically. Here, everything is based on *kāma*, desire, so real service is not possible in this plane.

There is no possibility of exploitation existing in the land of dedication, for every unit there is a dedicating one. In the lower portion of the land of dedication there is some calculation, some awe and reverence. But in the higher sphere, it is all automatic spontaneous love: a labor of love, with increased intensity and earnestness. And we are only charmed by the beauty and love that is found in Goloka Vṛndāvana, the supreme abode of Krishna. In a nutshell, this is what we understand by the grace of our spiritual masters. We are very much attracted by this conception which has been given to us by our *gurudeva* as he has received it from the Vedic scriptures, especially the *Śrīmad-Bhāgavatam*. This has been explained by Śrī Chaitanya Mahāprabhu Himself, by His teachings and practices, and this conception has been expounded by His followers, the Six Goswāmīs of Vṛndāvana.

# Six Philosophies of India

There are six ancient philosophical systems of India. The first is the *Vaiśeṣika* philosophy of Kaṇāda Ṛṣi: the atomic theory. According to him, everything is made of atoms. So many different atoms combine and produce this world. *Kaṇa* means atomic particle. So many atomic particles have combined and produced this world by chance, with no necessity of any reason, rhyme, consciousness, nothing of the kind. And the outcome of these combinations has produced what we find here. That is the opinion of Kaṇāda: it is an atomic world.

Bhaktivinoda Ṭhākur, the nineteenth century founder of the Krishna consciousness movement, sings in one song: *keśava! tuyā jagata vicitra*. "O my Lord Krishna, I see that everything is available in Your world, which has an infinite, variegated nature. Separated from You, however, we are always feeling miseries. A continuous flow of suffering has swallowed us from birth to death, and we cannot tolerate the pain of such misery. And so many relief agents: Kapila, Patañjali, Gautama, Kaṇāda, Jaimini, Buddha, are running towards us, offering their solutions."

## Analysis, Yoga, and Logic

Kapila has come with the *Sāṅkhya* philosophical system of analysis saying, "Analyze matter, and you will be free from all this pain." Patañjali has come with yoga, "Hey, *jīvātma!* Come to meet Paramātmā! Then all the problems of this world will go away from you. Come in connection with Paramātmā, the Supersoul." This is his recommendation .

Gautama comes with logic, *nyāya śāstra:* "There is one Maker, one Creator, but He is indifferent. He has created this world, finished, and left it. And you must try to live with the help of your reason. Develop your reasoning faculty, and be reasonable in all your conduct. Then only can you help yourself in this world. There is no other remedy. Be a good logician, and then you will be able to control the environment with the power of reason, and you will be happy." And Kaṇāda: "By chance atoms have been combined, and with the dissolution of atoms, nothing will remain. Why do you bother? Don't care. What is fate? It is nothing; ignore it. And when the body is dissolved, nothing will remain. Why lament?"

## Atomic Theory and Karma

Then, with the philosophy of *karma-mīmāṁsā*, Jaimini says, "There may be One who has connected us with this world and our *karma*, but *karma* is all in all. He is an indifferent observer. He has got no hold on us any longer. According to our *karma* we shall thrive or we shall go down. So, these activities are recommended to you. If you go on with your *karma* you will be happy. Of course, it cannot be denied; *karma phala*, the result of *karma*, diminishes and is ended. But stick to *karma*, good *karma*; don't go to bad *karma*. The result of good *karma* will be finished, but that does not matter; again go on doing good *karma*, and the good result will await you in heaven, and you will have a happy life. If anything is friendly to you, it is your *karma*. There is God, but He is indifferent. He is bound to serve you either good or bad, according to your *karma*. He has no independence."

## "DISSOLVE YOUR MIND"—BUDDHA

Then another class of philosophy is that of Buddha: "Only the combination of different things has created your mental system. With the dissolution of the mental system, nothing remains. So, somehow, we must dissolve the mental system. Practice *ahiṁsā*, nonviolence, *satya*, truthfulness, and so on."

It is seen that all these philosophers are talking either of renunciation or of exploitation *(bhukti, mukti)*. And by setting different types of enchanting traps, they arrange to capture the *jīva* soul. Bhaktivinoda Ṭhākur says, "But I have come to realize that these fellows are all cheaters. And they all have this common stand; they have no touch of Your devotion, Your service.

There, they are one. They cannot deliver any real good. They are common to oppose Your devotional service and supremacy. And ultimately they leave us in chaos.

"But from the ultimate standpoint, I see that they are agents engaged by You to segregate the seriously diseased persons to another ward, for the good of the less seriously diseased patients. It is Your arrangement to segregate the hopeless persons to another side for the benefit of the good side. That is Your design, and they are playing in Your hand like so many dolls. They are Your agents and they are also serving You in some way, because nothing is outside You." Bhaktivinoda Ṭhākur concludes saying, "I bid good-bye to them all. I feel in my heart that I shall show respect to all these so-called good agents from a distance, however, my only real capital is the dust of the holy feet of Your devotees. I rely on that dust as the source of all my prospects. I seek to put all my energy into taking the dust of their holy lotus feet upon my head. This is everything for me."

# BEYOND CHRISTIANITY

*In the following conversation, Śrīla Śrīdhar Mahārāj compares theistic beliefs with some Christian students from America.*

**Christian:** Can you explain the *Vaiṣṇava* viewpoint of Christianity?

**Śrīdhar Mahārāj:** Christianity is incomplete Vaiṣṇavism — not full-fledged, but the basis of devotional theism. We find the principle of "Die to live" there to a certain extent, at least physically. The Christians say that the ideal shown by Jesus is self-sacrifice. In our consideration, however, that is not full-fledged theism, but only the basis. It is an unclear, vague conception of Godhead: "We are for Him." But how much? And in what shape, in what attitude? All these things are unexplained and unclear in Christianity. Everything is hazy, as if seen from far off. It does not take any proper shape. The cover is not fully removed, allowing us to come face to face with the object of our service. The conception of service to God is there, and a strong impetus to attain that, so the foundation is good, but the structure over the foundation is unclear, vague, and imperfect.

**Christian:** Christians like the ideas of surrender, service, and giving everything to God.

**Śrīdhar Mahārāj:** Yes, that is common. But surrender to whom?

**Christian:** Christians say that Jesus is the only way.

**Śrīdhar Mahārāj:** Yes, and his way is "Die to live," but what for? What is our positive attainment? What is our positive engagement in the Lord's service? We must not only submit in gratefulness to the highest authority, but we must have a direct connection with Him, and cent percent engagement in His service. Simply going on in our own way, praying, "Oh God, give us our bread," going to the church once a week is not sufficient. Twenty-four hour engagement is possible in full-fledged theism. God can engage us twenty-four hours a day—we must attain that position: full engagement with Him. Everything else is subordinate to that position.

### ADAM AND EVE: FORCED TO LABOR

**Christian:** There are some Christian traditions that are very similar to Krishna consciousness.

**Śrīdhar Mahārāj:** They are very akin in their foundation. We agree that we must sacrifice everything for God. But who is He? And who am I? And what is our relationship? Christianity gives us only a hazy conception.

In the Christian conception, when Adam and Eve were surrendered, they had no problems in life. But then they tasted the fruit of the tree of knowledge, calculation of self-interest, and they fell, and were forced to live a life of labor. Only a general idea of our relationship with God is given there, but when we have to define in detail the characteristics of God, and in which relationships to approach Him, Christianity gives us only a hazy idea.

Once some Christian priests told our *guru mahārāj* that *mādhurya rasa* (conjugal relationship with God) is also found within Christianity. In the middle ages, there was a fashion amongst the Christians to consider Christ as a bridegroom, and some parable is also given where Lord Jesus Christ is considered as a bridegroom. So, they said that *mādhurya rasa*, the consort relationship, is also found within Christianity. Prabhupād told them, "That is with His Son, with His devotee; not with God." Son means *guru*, the deliverer.

## FATHER, SON, AND GHOST

Their conception of God is the Trinity: God the Father, God the Son, and God the Ghost. The Ghost is perhaps considered to have the highest position. If it is so, then Christianity ends in *brahmavāda nirviśeṣa*. Do you follow?

**Christian:** Yes. I think you explained before that *Brahman* means the impersonal aspect of God's existence.

**Śrīdhar Mahārāj:** God the Father means God the creator. God the Son is *guru*. And God as Ghost perhaps holds the supreme position in Christianity: over the Father conception, and over the Son conception. If that is the case, then their understanding goes to impersonal *Brahman*.

I was told that once in a drama in Germany, they had to show the figure of God, so in some high position in a balcony they put a figure of grave nature with a gray beard, commanding from there. God the Father was shown like that. That is their idea: the Fatherhood of Godhead, a gray-bearded, old man as God. But from the consideration of *rasa* and *ānanda*, ecstasy, God should be the center of all different relationships, including sonhood, and consorthood.

To conceive of God as our Father is an incomplete understanding, for parents are also servitors. He must be in the center; not in any extremity of the whole. He is not simply watching over the whole; the conception of Krishna is that of God in the center. Of all approaches to God, the approach for a loving relationship is supreme. The intensity of that relationship is to be considered, and God must be at the center of all loving relationships. *Ānandam brahmaṇo vidvān*. *Ānanda* is the most precious thing ever discovered. And the full representation of the highest *ānanda* should be considered as the highest absolute which can attract everyone: not by power, not by force, but by charm. The center of all attraction is Krishna. His attraction is by beauty, by charm, and by love — and not by coercion and force. That is the Krishna conception of Godhead.

**Christian:** Christians are afraid to go beyond Jesus, because Jesus has warned us about cheaters.

**Śrīdhar Mahārāj:** I am not speaking about the Christians;

The center of all atraction is Krishna. His attraction is by beauty, by charm, and by love — not by coercion and force.

I am speaking about Jesus, who has given the ideals of Christianity. I am speaking about the principles of Jesus. He has given some understanding by installments, but not full knowledge. We agree about the strong foundation of theism. Jesus was crucified because he said, "Everything belongs to my Father. Render unto Caesar that which is Caesar's, and render unto God that which is His." So, the foundation is very good; it is laudable, but that is only the first installment of the theistic conception.

Who is my Lord? What is His nature? Who am I? What is my inner self, and what is my connection with Him? How can I live continuously in His memory and service? The conception that we are meant for Him, designed and destined for Him, is laudable, but it must be clarified. We must attain the highest position. All these things are absent in Christianity. Only sacrifice for the Lord is given, and that is all right, it is the basic necessity of the soul. But after that, what is to be achieved? They are silent.

## BEYOND JESUS

**Christian:** They are afraid to go beyond Jesus.
**Śrīdhar Mahārāj:** Yes, but there is so much grace, so much love in divinity that God can sit on our lap and embrace us. A much more intimate connection is unfolded in Vaiṣṇavism. But if we are afraid to cross the fundamental advice of Jesus, then we become *sahajiyās* (imitationists). We must risk everything for our Lord and make our position firm in His service. We must die to live. And what is living? We have to analyze what real life is. And if without dying, we want to drag

God into our fleshy play, then we become *sahajiyās*, imitationists.

We must cross the threshold given by Jesus. He has declared, "Die to live." The Lord's company is so valuable to us that we must risk everything for Him. This material achievement is nothing; it is all poison. We must have no attraction for it. We must be ready to leave everything, all our material prospects and aspirations, including our body, for Him. God is great. But what is His greatness? What is my position? How can I engage myself in His service twenty-four hours a day? Here, Jesus is silent.

We receive no specific program from the Christians at this stage, so Vaiṣṇavism comes to our heart's relief, to satisfy our inner necessity, whatever it may be. Our inner thirst will be quenched there. You may be conscious or unconscious of the many demands within you, but they will reach full satisfaction in its most beautiful form there alone. It is not only that from far off we shall show God some reverential salute, but we can have Him in a very intimate way. The ideal of an intimate loving connection with God has been given by Vaiṣṇavism, especially by Śrī Chaitanya Mahāprabhu, by *Śrīmad-Bhāgavatam*, and in Vṛndāvana, the land of Krishna.

The feeling of possessing anything here in the material world cannot be real; it is a perverted reflection, but that feeling must be present in the original world, otherwise what is its origin? From where do the different feelings of necessity within us come? They must be present in the causal world, for everything is emanating from Krishna. So, the hankering of every atom of our body, mind, and soul will receive its greatest fulfillment there. This understanding is given by Vaiṣṇavism, by Śrī Chaitanya Mahāprabhu, by *Śrīmad-Bhāgavatam*, and by Krishna in the *Bhagavad-gītā*.

## BHAGAVAD-GĪTĀ: ITS HISTORY AND TEACHINGS

**Christian:** I've heard of the *Bhagavad-gītā*. What is the history of its origin?
**Śrīdhar Mahārāj:** In the *Bhagavad-gītā*, Krishna tells Arjuna, "What I am saying to you now is not a new thing. I have already told this to Sūrya, the sun-god, and he delivered it to Manu, the father of man. In this way, this knowledge descended in disciplic succession, and by the influence of time it was finished. Again, I am repeating that ancient knowledge to you."

This refers to *karma-yoga*: "Don't care about the result, good or bad; go on with your duty. Then you can have general peace of mind."
**Christian:** What is the message of the *Bhagavad-gītā?*
**Śrīdhar Mahārāj:** There are different stages of education imparted in *Bhagavad-gītā*: *bhakti-yoga*, *karma-yoga*, *jñāna-yoga*, *aṣṭānga-yoga*, so many different layers of theism, but pure devotional theism begins where Krishna says, *sarva-dharmān parityajya* "Give up your affinity to all other

activities, whether religious or nonreligious, and wholly surrender to Me. Don't try to push your demands on Me, but ask Me what will be most beneficial for you. And what shall I do on your behalf? Fully surrender to Me, and I will give Myself to you."

"All these other methods and their prospects are more or less effective and valuable, but don't aspire after anything but Me. That will be your highest prospect; to want Me, to have Me, to live in Me, to do what I say, to enter into My own personal family in my private life. That will be your highest attainment. Don't aspire for anything else from Me. The comparative study of all religious aspirations will show that the highest inner necessity may be satisfied by entrance into My personal private dealings."

**Christian:** Christians think that if we are to be sincere, we should follow the Bible. We take very literally the word of Christ.

**Śrīdhar Mahārāj:** Yes, according to one's capacity he may be enlisted in a particular class. Some will go to Christianity, and after finishing that, if their hankering is still unsatisfied, they will seek somewhere else, thinking, "What is God? I want to know more perfectly."

In this regard, I can give one example: there was a Professor Nixon in England. He went to fight against Germany in the First World War, on the French side. As he was flying over the German lines, his airplane was hit, and began to fall. He saw that the plane would fall on the German lines. When I met him here in India, he told me, "At that time, I prayed, 'If there is any God, let Him save me, and I promise that if I do not die in this plane crash, I will go to search after Him. I will devote my whole life in search of Him.'"

The plane crashed, and when Professor Nixon regained consciousness, he found that he was behind the French lines, in a hospital in France. At that time, He thought to himself, "There is God! He has heard my last prayer." When his wounds were healed, he went straight to England to see some churchmen. He told them, "I want to search after God, and engage myself twenty-four hours a day in the cause of His service. I want to see Him face to face."

## BISHOPS: "GO TO INDIA"

He saw many clergymen and even some bishops, and they ultimately advised him, "If you want to see God face to face, then go to India. We cannot recommend such a process to you. But we have heard that in India there are *yogīs* who internally connect with the Lord in the heart. You may try your fortune there." So, he came here to India, where he met the Vice-Chancellor of Lucknow University. In talking with him, Professor Nixon met the Vice-Chancellor's wife, who was a Gauḍīya Vaiṣṇava, a devotee of Mahāprabhu. He was so much charmed by her advice that he accepted her as his *guru*. Finally he took *sannyās* (the renounced order of life), and his name became Swāmī Krishna Prema. He established a temple here in India, and preached about *bhāgavata-dharma*, and Mahāprabhu.

He made a comparative study of all religions, beginning from Christianity, and gradually came to Vaiṣṇavism, attracted by Mahāprabhu's gift. One German scholar also said, "In all the religious conceptions of the world, the conception of twenty-four hour engagement with God *(aṣṭakālīya-līlā)* has never been given. I have studied all religious theologies, but none could even conceive of twenty-four hour service to the Supreme Lord. It is only given in *Śrīmad-Bhāgavatam*."

Rūpa Goswāmī has given the scientific representation of Krishna: *akhila-rasāmṛta-mūrtiḥ*. He is the reservoir of all possible pleasures. All possible tendencies for satisfaction that we may feel, and even those that we may not feel are present in Krishna and have their ideal, purest satisfaction with Him alone. He is all-accommodating and all-comprehensive. Whatever satisfaction our inner heart demands can be fulfilled only by Him.

**Christian:** Some Christians are so much afraid to go beyond the Bible that they will not make a study of other theistic beliefs.

**Śrīdhar Mahārāj:** According to one's capacity, he will purchase in the market *(sve sve 'dhikare ya niṣṭha sa guṇaḥ parikīrtitaḥ)*. In the market, there may be valuable things, but the buyer must have some capacity to purchase them. The *ṛṣis*, the tradesmen of knowledge have also gone so far as to say, "This is the highest. Go no further." Similarly, Krishna says in the *Bhagavad-gītā (3.35), svadharme nidhanaṁ śreyaḥ para-dharmo bhayāvahaḥ:* "Don't go ahead—you'll be doomed. Take your stand here; go no further."

Why is such a great warning given to us? Generally our teachers advise us, "Pay full attention here. Only then will you understand everything completely, and your march to the end-point will be sincere and satisfactory. Otherwise, *sahajiyāism*, imitationism will enter your heart. Do you think that in one leap you can capture the summit of a hill? Impossible. You must march, but your march must be sincere. You must make real progress, not imitative progress." This warning is given at every stage of life. "This is the highest for you. Give your whole attention to this. Don't be absent-minded and haphazard in your study. Engage yourself fully in this lesson, and the next higher stage will come to you automatically."

As a matter of policy, we are told that our present stage of instruction is the highest. When a professor comes to teach a child, he will accept the mentality of the child. He will say, "Only go so far, and no further. This is the final stage; give your whole attention to understanding this point, and when that is finished, then go further." In this way, by gradual installments, knowledge is revealed.

**Christian:** So, there are different stages for different persons?

**Śrīdhar Mahārāj:** Bhaktivinoda Ṭhākur has given his decision, in his *Tattva-sūtra*, that although when *Bhagavad-gītā* was spoken to Arjuna, he engaged himself in fighting, had it been Uddhava in place of Arjuna, after hearing the conclusion of *Bhagavad-gītā* where Krishna says, "Give up everything and surrender to Me," Uddhava would have accepted this and gone away from the warfield. Upon hearing the same advice, Arjuna acted in one way, but Uddhava would have acted in another. After hearing the first installment of Krishna's instructions Arjuna tells Krishna in the *Bhagavad-gītā* (3.1-2):

**jyāyasī cet karmaṇas te**
**matā buddhir janārdana**
**tat kiṁ karmaṇi ghore māṁ**
**niyojayasi keśava**

**vyāmiśreṇeva vākyena**
**buddhiṁ mohayasīva me**
**tad ekaṁ vada niścitya**
**yena śreyo 'ham āpnuyām**

"You say that *jñāna*, knowledge, is better than *karma*, work. Why then do you want to engage me in this dreadful *karma* of fighting?" Then Krishna said, "You have your capacity in *karma:* finish your career, and then you can aspire to come to the level of *jñāna*, inquiry into knowledge. It is not a cheap thing to transcend all activity and attain *naiṣkarmya*, freedom from *karma*. First finish the course of your *karma*; then you will become free from *karma*, and gradually you will develop transcendental knowledge and devotion. So, I say, 'Engage yourself in this present fight.' Fighting is not recommended for everyone, but for you, and men of your section."

**Christian:** In your opinion, what stage of God realization should people be advised to follow?

**Śrīdhar Mahārāj:** Krishna consciousness should be preached in a general way; and people will come according to their inner response. Some may even come to attack us. The communists will say, "No religious preaching is allowed here. It is all theoretical; you neglect the concrete world, and take the abstract to be everything. By hearing this, the people will suffer, so we won't allow it." That is one stage. Beginning from there, there are so many stages. If you preach to a crowd, those who find a response within their inner hearts will come to you according to the degree of their realization. Their inner demand will bring them in contact with an agent of truth.

Bhaktivedanta Swāmī Mahārāj went to the West and preached, and so many converted to Krishna consciousness. How was it possible? They were not Gauḍīya Vaiṣṇavas, but they felt some inner affinity. While wandering in this world, everyone is gathering some new experience, some new taste. According to the degree of his awakenment, one will respond to a preacher in his own layer. He will find, "Oh! After so long, I see that there is the possibility of an outlet for the urge I found in my heart. There is a plane that can satisfy that aspiration of mine. I must connect with him and inquire of that land of my dreams." In this way, they will come to seek the association of devotees. "Birds of a feather flock together." According to their inner taste, they will come together and go on with their duties in that plane, at that pace, until from there they can go further, to a higher position. Sometimes in the same life one may change his creed and go higher, and sometimes one may wait until his next birth.

**Christian:** If the quality of preaching is too high, people may be discouraged.

**Śrīdhar Mahārāj:** It may be too high for one and too near for another. It is not too high for all, for if it was, then how would conversion be possible? So many people are becoming Mohammedans, Christians, and Hindus. All Christians were not born Christians. How were people first attracted to become Christians? There arose in their hearts the hankering for Christianity.

When Acyutānanda Swāmī, the first disciple of Bhaktivedanta Swāmī Mahārāj, went to my birthplace here in Bengal, a headmaster asked him, "We are so near and we cannot appreciate the teachings of Śrī Chaitanya Mahāprabhu; how is it that from such a far off country, you have come to sacrifice your life for the service of Śrī Chaitanyadeva?"

Acyutananda Swāmī answered, "*Brahmāṇḍa bhrahmite kona bhāgyavān jīva.* We have to acquire this

We must cross the threshold given by Jesus Christ. He has declared, "Die to live."

capacity during the course of our wanderings in different positions throughout the creation."

We are wandering from this land to that land, from this species to that species, and in the course of that, we gather some *sukṛti*, pious credits. *Ajñāta-sukṛti* means that unknowingly and unconsciously our energy is spent in the service of the Lord, and the reaction comes in the form of some pious credits. And when *sukṛti* is more developed, it becomes *jñāta-sukṛti*, or pious activities knowingly performed. Then, *śraddhā*, faith, our inner attraction for the universal truth comes to the surface. In this way it may develop from any stage. Even a beast may feel the tendency to serve Krishna. In Vṛndāvana, so many living beings; trees, beasts, and even the water have acquired their position by consciously desiring it. Although they have accepted an apparently material pose, they eternally hold that position in the service of Krishna.

## WAY OF THE PILGRIM

**Christian:** There is one book called *The Way of The Pilgrim*, about a Christian who chants the name of Jesus on beads.

**Śrīdhar Mahārāj:** Yes, the Catholics also use beads. Some Christians may chant the name of Christ.

**Christian:** This man was chanting the name of Jesus, his heart was growing soft, and he was feeling ecstasy, great love for Jesus.

**Śrīdhar Mahārāj:** Then he may attain the position of Jesus, at most. It may be that in his attempt for perfection, his growth is finished there, in the eternal paraphernalia of Jesus. He may remain there. If he has found his fullest satisfaction, he is fated to be there.

By the will of God, and by the powerful will of an exalted devotee, even from the impersonal *Brahman* effulgence one may be roused from his slumber and moved to action in devotional service. Generally, they pass long ages there in the nondifferentiated plane, satisfied with their spiritual attainment; however, in the consideration of infinite time, nothing is very great or spacious. They may remain holding that position for a long time, so many dissolutions and creations may come and go, but the possibility remains that their slumber may be broken at any time. Since time immemorial, this created world has been in existence, and so many souls are ascending to the *Brahman* effulgence and again descending. So, even in the midst of the infinite *Brahman* effulgence, some souls are coming out. It is a question of infinity, so the position of Jesus may be considered as eternal, and the time may come when Jesus himself may be converted into Vaiṣṇavism. It is not impossible.

## JESUS: DYNAMIC OR STATIC?

**Christian:** Do you think that Jesus had awareness of Krishna as the Personality of Godhead?
**Śrīdhar Mahārāj:** When his inner attainment is most closely detected, then we are bound to say that in the course of his eternal life, there is some possibility of his achieving Krishna.
**Christian:** I don't understand.
**Śrīdhar Mahārāj:** Is Jesus stagnant or progressive?

Where he has reached, is that finished forever, or is he dynamic?

**Christian:** Christians will say that he has full knowledge.

**Śrīdhar Mahārāj:** So, is he stagnant there, finally fixed? Is that Jesus' position? Do the bishops say that his position is final? Does he have a progressive life? Or is Jesus alone barred from making further progress? Is he a member of the dynamic world? Or the stagnant world?

So, this is the nature of the infinite. Being finite, we are going to deal with the infinite? That is our ludicrous tendency. It is ludicrous for us to deal with the infinite.

Why is Krishna considered to be the Absolute Truth? This you should inquire about in a scientific way, step by step. As I have recommended, you should go on reading about that in the *Śrī Krishna Saṁhitā*, and the *Bṛhad Bhāgavatāmṛta. You* should try to follow very minutely the dynamic development of theism as it is presented there.

## REINCARNATION—TRANSMIGRATION

**Christian:** As I understand it, reincarnation means that a soul may regress into a lower species by performing sinful acts. But how does it benefit a soul to be punished by taking birth in the animal species if later he has no recollection of this?

**Śrīdhar Mahārāj:** Sometimes it is necessary for doctors to make a patient unconscious. Sometimes a *dacoit* is imprisoned and put under chains. When his movements will be detrimental to society, he is confined in a cell and chained. So, sometimes it is necessary to take away one's independence, his voluntary action. By suffering the reactions to his previous *karma*, one may be relieved; then again he may be given voluntary action. When by his voluntary will a soul has done so many misdeeds and acquired so many reactions, it is necessary that his freewill be stopped temporarily. He will be allowed to suffer the reactions of his previous sins, and then again some freedom will be given to him so that he may take the proper course which is useful for him. As long as a drunkard is a drunkard, when he is expected to do some mischief to the environment, he should be confined. And when the madness of drinking is gone, then he will be released and allowed to move freely.

### "Do Unto Others" Includes Animals

**Christian:** Christians generally don't accept that animals have souls.

**Śrīdhar Mahārāj:** Jesus did not care to bring his followers within that conception. He saw that they were accustomed to eating animals and fish, so he did not want to embarrass them with all these questions. He thought they should begin theistic life, and when again they are able to consider these points, at that time they may be given this installment.

Life is also present within the nonhuman species, and it is no less qualified than the human position, but in the course of the evolutionary movement of the soul, it is thrown into such a condition as the result of *karma*. Wherever life is present, the soul is there within. It is a common thing, but Jesus thought it would be impossible for them to adjust their understanding of the environment to such a degree. He thought to let them begin with the culture of theism, and then gradually such instruction could be given.

He told them, "Do unto others as you would have them do unto you." That is also good. But not only is the soul present there; God is also there, and everywhere. The lower species are also feeling pain and pleasure. In animals it is quite clear that when they are killed, they feel pain. So, there is life. The vibration of pain is there, consciousness is there, and the soul is a unit of pure consciousness. But the persons to whom Jesus preached were not so qualified as to extend their knowledge that far. They are not prepared for such a great amount of sacrifice in their practices. So, for those who are not prepared to sacrifice themselves to such an extent, Christianity has been given by Jesus.

Still, everything has been ordained from the same common center. Christianity has its necessity, Islam also has its necessity. There is room for such creeds in the universe. They are not unnecessary, but they hold a relative position.

Then what is the position of the Absolute Truth? When we have to inquire deeply about this, then we come to India. There it has been dealt with very extensively, with all possible conceptions of religion. So many variegated theological conceptions are found in India that a fraction of that cannot be found anywhere else in the world. But ultimately, *Śrīmad-Bhāgavatam* was given as the highest conception. How? That we have to understand and follow very minutely. You should study the *Bṛhad Bhāgavatāmṛta* and its more modern form, *Śrī Krishna Saṁhitā* by Bhaktivinoda Ṭhākur.

**Christian:** I have read that.

**Śrīdhar Mahārāj:** But you must read it more closely, and more scrutinizingly. You must read that again and again, until you find satisfaction, and answers to all your inquiries. There, the gradation of our relationship with God is shown, explaining how from a particular stage of theism, one is forced to progress to a higher level of attainment.

# Levels of God Realization

The gradation of transcendental realization has been explained by Śrīla Sanātan Goswāmī in his book *Bṛhad Bhāgavatāmṛta* There we find that in the course of the realization of *śuddha-bhakti*, pure devotional service, the great sage Nārada Muni is visiting different places. First, he encounters *karma-miśra bhakti*, or devotional service mixed with fruitive activities.

Once there was a *brāhmaṇa* in Allahabad. He was a wealthy man, and on the occasion of the *Kumbha-mela*, when millions of sages and devotees gather for a religious festival, he arranged for services to the different types of saintly persons who were present there. He conducted a sacrifice and finally finished the function with the chanting of the holy name of the Lord. The *brāhmaṇa* was mainly engaged in *karma-kaṇda*, or fruitive work, but he was also rendering service to the saintly persons. Ultimately he ended everything with *nāma-saṅkīrtan*, the chanting of the holy names of the Lord.

Nārada Muni approached the *brāhmaṇa* saying, "You are very fortunate that you are doing these things. This is the proper utilization of your money and caste. By engaging in such holy activities, you are certainly most fortunate." The *brāhmaṇa* told him, "What am I doing? This is nothing. You should go to see the fortune of King Indradyumna. He is distributing the *prasāda* remnants of Lord Jagannāth in a grand style. How grandiose is the worship of Nārāyaṇa there! Go there, and you will appreciate his devotional service.

So, Nārada Muni went to see Indradyumna Mahārāj, and there he also found the king extensively engaging all his resources in the worship of Lord Jagannāth. Nārada approached him, saying, "You are so fortunate in this world." The king told him, "What can I do Nārada? This is nothing. If you want to see how devotional service should be practiced, you should go to Lord Indra, the king of heaven.

Nārada Muni went to Indradeva and praised him by saying, "O Indra, you are very fortunate. Vāmanadeva, the Supreme Personality of Godhead, appeared as your younger brother. And here in Indraloka, there are always religious festivals worshiping Krishna." Indra said, "Oh, what do you say? What love have I for Krishna? Everything belongs to Him, but in my foolishness, I tried to prevent Him from taking the *pārijāta* tree from heaven. Not only that, but I am always being attacked by the demons, and my wife is also sometimes disturbed; what fortune do you find in me?"

From Indra, Nārada went to Lord Brahmā, the creator of the universe. There he found the personified

South Indian relief of Lord Brahmā, the creator of the universe (left), and Lord Śiva, the universal destroyer (right).

*Vedas* singing praise to Lord Brahmā. Nārada, who was also his son and disciple, approached Lord Brahmā saying, "How greatly fortunate you are! You are entrusted by Lord Nārāyaṇa Himself with the management of the whole universe, and sometimes you visit Him for guidance in the administration of the universe. We also find that some portions of the *Vedas* are engaged in singing your glories. You are so fortunate!"

Lord Brahmā felt a little disturbed. He said, "What are you saying, Nārada? You are praising me and increasing my false pride, but did I not tell you that I am nothing but a small creature in the hand of Nārāyaṇa? I am engaged in external activity. I have no time to give in the interest of my devotional life. My Lord has rather deceived me by engaging me in such a busy matter as managing the universe. I am most unfortunate. Rather, you should go to Mahādeva, Lord Śiva. He does not care for anything in this world. He is aloof and indifferent, and has his aim toward Lord Nārāyaṇa. He is devoted to Lord Rāmacandra, and he is very fond of the holy name of Lord Rāma. His wife, Pārvatī devi, is also helping him in his devotional life, and she is very happy.

Nārada Muni went to Śivaloka and began to chant in praise of Lord Śiva, "You are the master of the world. The *Vedas* sing your glories. You hold the highest position." In this way, Nārada began to glorify him, but Lord Śiva became very excited and a little angry at this: "What are you saying, Nārada? I have so much indifference towards this world that I am mainly interested in knowledge and penance. This holds the better portion of my interest. Whatever little inclination I have for devotional service to Nārāyaṇa is very negligible. Sometimes I have such an apathetic spirit towards Nārāyaṇa that I even fight with Him in favor of one of my disciples! I am disgusted with my position. Penance, power, mystic yoga perfection, and indifference to the world: that is my business."

This is *jñāna-miśra bhakti*, or devotional service mixed with empiric speculative knowledge. Lord Brahmā is the ideal of *karma-miśra bhakti*, or devotional service mixed with fruitive activity, and Lord Śiva is the ideal of *jñāna-miśra bhakti*. He still maintains some affinity for an independent position, and not for cent-per-cent acceptance of service to the Supreme Lord, Nārāyaṇa.

Lord Śiva said, "If you really want to experience *śuddha-bhakti*, go to Prahlāda Mahārāj. There you will find pure devotional service."

In this way, we have been directed to trace the development of *śuddha-bhakti*, pure devotional service, beginning with Prahlāda Mahārāj, because Prahlāda does not want anything in exchange for his devotional service.

In *Śrīmad-Bhāgavatam* (7.10.4.) he says:

**nānyathā te 'khila-guro**
**ghaṭeta karuṇātmanaḥ**
**yas ta āśiṣa āśāste**
**na sa bhṛtyaḥ sa vai vaṇik**

"Whoever is doing something for the satisfaction of Nārāyaṇa and wants something in return, is not a servant, but a merchant. He wants to give something to the Lord and then take some price in exchange for that." So, Prahlāda Mahārāj is a pure devotee, and only through a pure devotee of Nārāyaṇa can one attain pure devotion.

## NEUTRAL LOVE OF GOD

All these peculiar achievements in the devotional world begin with Prahlāda Mahārāj. The nature of his devotional service is that of *śānta rasa*, neutrality, where there is no actual service, but only perfect adherence to Nārāyaṇa under all circumstances. Whatever may be the unfavorable condition in the environment, he stands true to the faith that Nārāyaṇa is all in all, and that He is our master. So, Prahlāda Mahārāj, and the four Kumāras, the sons of Lord Brahmā, are in the position of *śānta rasa bhakti*, or neutral love of God.

Prahlāda Mahārāj is Nārada Muni's disciple. Still, for our benefit, Nārada Muni was approaching him to measure the standard of his devotion in a comparative study of the devotional world. Approaching Prahlāda Mahārāj, Nārada said, "I have come to see you, Prahlāda, because Lord Śiva also appreciates your position. You are really a devotee of Lord Krishna. You are so fortunate! I have come to see how you are."

Prahlāda Mahārāj told him, "*Gurudeva*, you are all in all. Have you come to test me? Whatever fortune I may have, I have received by your grace. I was born in a family of demons, so the demonic qualities have not exclusively left me. Don't you know that in Naimiṣāraṇya, I went to fight with Lord Viṣṇu? I repent for that, but what can I do? He has given me such a position. I cannot have the privilege of direct service to Him, but only mentally I think of Him. I think that He is everything, but I do not have the great fortune of rendering service to Him. Hanumān is really a devotee. How fortunate he is! What grace he has received! He gave everything to Lord Rāmacandra. I envy his situation, but what can I do? God's dispensation is absolute. We must accept that. Hanumān's position is really enviable. How attached to his master he is, and what a great magnitude of service he has done for Lord Rāma."

## HANUMĀN: SERVANT OF RĀMA

From there, Nārada Muni went to visit Hanumān. He approached Hanumān's residence, playing on his *vina* the *mantram: Rāma Rāma Rāma Rāma Rāma.* When Hanumān suddenly heard the name of his master, Lord Rāma, he jumped towards that direction, and even in the sky, embraced Nārada Muni. Hanumān said, "Oh, who is helping me to hear the sound of Lord Rāma's holy name? After such a long time, the sound of Rāma *nāma* is enlivening me. I was dying without hearing the name of Rāma." Ecstatic tears were running down the eyes of both of them. Then Nārada Muni went to Hanumān's quarters, and began to praise his fortune, saying, "How fortunate you are! Oh, Hanumān, You serve Lord Rāmacandra so intimately; you do not know anything

Deity of Hanumān, the devoted servant of Lord Rāmacandra.

but your master, Lord Rāma. You rendered such great service to Him that your service has become the ideal for the whole of human society."

Hanumān told Nārada, "Yes, by His grace I was able to do something, but it is all His grace; I am nothing, I am worthless. But I hear that now Lord Rāmacandra has come as Lord Krishna. Although I don't like any incarnation other than Lord Rāma, I have heard from a distance how Krishna, who is Rāmacandra Himself, is showing His favor to the Pāṇḍavas. The Pāṇḍavas are very fortunate because the Lord is dealing with them like an intimate friend. So, I have great appreciation for the fortune of the Pāṇḍavas. "In this way, Hanumān began to praise the Pāṇḍavas for their fortune.

## KRISHNA'S FRIENDS, THE PĀṆḌAVAS

Leaving Hanumān, Nārada Muni then went to the Pāṇḍavas. There he found Yudhiṣṭhira Mahārāj seated on a throne and began to sing the glories of the Pāṇḍavas. He told Yudhiṣṭhira Mahārāj, "How friendly you are in your relationship with Krishna! How fortunate you are!" Yudhiṣṭhira Mahārāj said, "What are you saying Devarṣi? Of course Krishna favors us, we can't deny that, but what is our position? We have no position at all. On the other hand, I feel now and then, that by seeing our example the people in general won't want to serve Krishna, because they will calculate that being such intimate friends of Lord Krishna, the Pāṇḍavas had to pass through difficult troubles and dangers their whole lives. They will think that to be a devotee of Krishna means that one must suffer troubles throughout his whole life. So, I am afraid that by thinking of us, people will not venture to approach Krishna."

Devarṣi Nārada said, "No, no, I don't see it from that angle of vision. What is danger or affliction to the Pāṇḍavas? What is the meaning of that? That is the message that Krishna is coming. When the Pāṇḍavas are in danger that is nothing but the message that Krishna is coming to save you. So, your mother also prayed:

**vipadaḥ santu tāḥ śaśvat**
**tatra tatra jagad-guro**
**bhavato darśanaṁ yat syād**
**apunar bhava-darśanam**

"'Let dangers come: may they visit me always. I don't care for that, because that brings Krishna much closer to us. We rather like the dangers that bring Krishna into our intimate connection.' That famous statement of your mother, Kuntīdevī, stands there."

The Pāṇḍavas, headed by Mahārāj Yudhiṣṭhira said, "Yes, Krishna visits us now and then, in the time of our dire need, but how fortunate are the Yadus! Lord Krishna is always with them. They are so proud of their master, Lord Krishna, that they do not care for any other power in the world. They are so fortunate that Lord Krishna is always closely connected with them." So, Nārada Muni went to the Yadus and began chanting in praise of them. They said, "What do you say, Devarṣi Nārada? Krishna is with us, of course, and in any time of great danger He comes to help us, but how much do we care for Him? We are living independently, careless about His existence. But among us, Uddhava is really His favorite. Whatever Krishna does, He always consults with Uddhava, and in all His confidential matters, Uddhava is present there, and in every case, He is always very thick with Uddhava. Even we envy the fortune of Uddhava."

## UDDHAVA: MORE DEAR THAN KRISHNA

Then Nārada went to Uddhava and told him, "Uddhava, you are the most favorite devotee of Krishna. Krishna says:

**na tathā me priyatama**
**ātma-yonir na śaṅkaraḥ**
**na ca saṅkarṣaṇo na śrīr**
**naivātmā ca yathā bhavān**

"'O Uddhava! What to speak of other devotees like Brahmā, Śiva, Saṅkarṣaṇa, or Lakṣmī; you are more dear to Me than My own life.' You are such an intimate associate that Krishna values you more than His own life." Uddhava said, "Yes, of course, out of His causeless benevolence, He might have said something like that, but I don't think that I am His real devotee, especially after visiting Vṛndāvana. All my pride has been melted by seeing those devotees. The spirit of service and the intensity of love towards Krishna that I found in the devotees in Vṛndāvana is unparalleled. O Devarṣi, I am nowhere. Do you know that statement of mine? It is recorded in the *Śrīmad Bhāgavatam* (10.47.61):

**āsām aho caraṇa-reṇu-juṣām ahaṁ syāṁ**
**vṛndāvane kim api gulma-latauṣadhīnām**
**yā dustyajaṁ sva-janam ārya-pathaṁ ca hitvā**
**bhejur mukunda-padavīṁ śrutibhir vimṛgyām**

"The *gopīs* of Vṛndāvana gave up their husbands, children, and families who are difficult to renounce, and sacrificed even their religious principles to take shelter of the lotus feet of Krishna, which are sought after even by the *Vedas* themselves. O! Grant me the fortune to take birth as a blade of grass in Vṛndāvana, so that I may take the dust of the lotus feet of those great souls upon my head.

"There I have disclosed my heart fully. The quality of love for Krishna that I found in the damsels of Vṛndāvana is so exalted that I could not but aspire to be born in Vṛndāvana as a piece of grass, so that the foot-dust of those divine damsels might touch my head. So, what are you saying Devarṣi? If you would like to see real devotion, real divine love, you should go to Vṛndāvana. Don't put us in an awkward position, saying that we possess devotion to Krishna; this is rather a mockery, a foundationless utterance. I found real devotees of the Lord in Vṛndāvana."

In this way, Sanātan Goswāmī tries his best to take us through the path, by showing us the gradual development of devotion to Krishna. Prahlāda Mahārāj has been accepted as the basis of *śuddha-bhakti*, the beginning of pure devotional service, because he is situated in *śānta rasa*, or devotional service in neutrality. Above that there is *dāsya rasa*, love of God in servitude, as shown by Hanumān, and above that there is *sakhya rasa*, or the mood of friendship. That is exemplified by the Pāṇḍavas. Uddhava is somewhat *sakhya*, connecting with *vātsalya*, parental love, and *mādhurya*, conjugal love. In this way we can trace the progressive development of devotion.

Our close adherence to Krishna develops in this way to Vṛndāvana. The acme of devotional service is found there. In the conversation between Rāmānanda Rāya and Śrī Chaitanya Mahāprabhu we find it mentioned that Rādhārāṇī's devotional service is categorically higher than that of the *gopīs* (*tebhyas tāḥ paśu-pāla-paṅkaja-dṛśas tābhyo 'pi sā rādhikā)*. The kind of serving spirit we find there is unaccountable and inconceivable.

Śrī Chaitanya Mahāprabhu came with *that* quality of adherence to the truth: unconditional surrender. He came seeking that fortune of serving the truth. If we can seek such a higher type of existence, we may consider ourselves most fortunate.

Self-surrender is the very basis of our highest fortune. We cannot but surrender ourselves to whatever beautiful and valuable thing we have come across. Our appreciation for any higher thing is shown by the degree of our surrender to that. So, we can measure the quality of the truth we are connected with only by the intensity of our surrender.

# The Krishna Conception

Surrender is not a lip transaction. Surrender means not only to surrender one's possessions, but to realize that the possessions themselves are false. I am not a master of anything. I am not even master of myself. Surrender means to give everything to the *guru*, and rid ourselves of the unholy connection of so many possessions, so that they may not disturb us by always suggesting, "You are my master," and in this way misleading us.

We should think, "Everything belongs to the Lord and His delegation, the *guru*. I am not the master of anything." That sort of knowledge we should imbibe, and that will be helpful to our real spiritual progress. This is reality. We have to realize that fact. We want the truth, and we want to free ourselves from false notions. So, proper *dīkṣā*, spiritual initiation, imparts the divine knowledge that nothing belongs to us; not only that, but everything belongs to God, including ourselves. That is the conception of *dīkṣā*: "I belong to Him; everything belongs to Him. I am His servant, and these are the objects of His service."

## FOOL'S PARADISE

This is reality, and we are suffering under non-reality in an imaginary world. We are living in a fool's paradise. We should do away with the fool's paradise and try to enter into real paradise. When we have a peep into the characteristic of the absolute environment of reality, and even a little regard for the truth, we can no longer relish the paraphernalia of this world as we did previously. Because we have had a real taste of the higher truth, we will have no charm for this material world. We will no longer feel encouragement to meet with the duties that are relating to this world of enjoyment. We will be indifferent.

We know that the connection with the present enjoying mood brings a painful reaction. We can realize that, but we cannot leave it behind. We cannot cut off the connection completely in the stage of *sādhana*, spiritual practice. Still, we have no other alternative. Our affinity for the positive truth should be increased more and more, and gradually our affinity for our paraphernalia and obligations will all disappear. Although repeatedly we may not be successful, still we will be unable to give up the idea. We will attempt again and again to make progress towards the truth, and when we are unsuccessful, our heart will ache to think that we are repeatedly being defeated by the enemies who are all around us.

## MENTAL MUSHROOMS

But the fire of Krishna consciousness is there, and that fire is not to be quenched. It is a spark of eternal truth. So, the fire will continue, and the day will come when the enemies that are surrounding us will have to retire once and for all. One day we will find that Krishna has gradually captured our whole heart, and the others have retired forever; they are no longer present to trouble us in our mental circle. We will find that those unwanted things were like mushrooms; they came out from our mental soil, and now they have all gone and died. They have all gone away, and Krishna alone is in the heart. At that time, the heart is only full of Krishna, full of the Krishna conception.

Śrīla Bhaktisiddhānta Saraswatī Ṭhākur once instructed a disciple at the time of initiation into the Hare Krishna *mantra* that Krishna should be allowed to land in our hearts, just as an army is landed by the navy. An army is carried by a ship, and when they have landed, the fight begins, and they capture the country, just as Julius Caesar said, "*Veni vidi vici*, I came, I saw, I conquered." So, we have to allow Krishna to land in our hearts. Then the fight will begin.

What is the proposal of Krishna consciousness, and what is the proposal of so many other conceptions? They are all giving us their assurances from time immemorial, saying, "I shall give you this, I shall give you that," but the Krishna conception will enter and say, "My claim is this: the whole thing is Mine, and you are all trespassers." The fight will begin; the unwanted things are sure to withdraw, and Krishna consciousness will capture the whole heart. This is the process. Krishna consciousness has only to land within our hearts. Somehow or other, from a pure devotee, a bit of real Krishna consciousness should enter through our ears into our hearts, and Krishna will supply whatever is required. One who has imbibed even a slight regard for Krishna consciousness is assured of success in spiritual life, today or tomorrow.

## KRISHNA IS A THIEF

We may have erected high walls on all sides to protect ourselves so that Krishna consciousness may not enter, but Krishna is a thief, and a thief requires no invitation. No preparation is necessary for His welcome. He will enter for His own interest, and that is our consolation. Our solace is that Krishna is a thief. *Māyā* has erected her high walls on all sides, but nothing is sufficient to stop Krishna consciousness. Krishna is a thief, and stealthily He will enter one day.

A devotee may become hopeless, thinking, "The enemy is within my own house; my own kinsmen are my enemies. I am hopeless." We may become disappointed, but Krishna consciousness will not leave us in any way. Krishna will persevere, and in due course of time, He will conquer. And other things, no matter how closely related they may be in private and well-protected rooms in our hearts, will have to go. They must take leave from every corner of our hearts. Krishna will conquer. Krishna will capture the whole thing. The unwanted lusty desires of our heart are foreign things. They are only mushrooms. Like mushrooms, they come out; they have no permanent stability or root. They are not rooted to the soil. We may think that what we have stored in our hearts is very near and dear, and that is already mixed with us as a part of our existence, but when Krishna consciousness enters, that will all float like mushrooms.

After all, they are mushrooms; they have no footing, no connection with the soil. They are only floating. All material interests are only floating on the surface. They are not deeply rooted within and without the whole of our existence. Only Krishna consciousness is present everywhere, within all parts of our existence. So, the mushrooms will have to vanish one day. This is confirmed in *Śrīmad-Bhāgavatam* (2.8.5):

**praviṣṭaḥ karṇa-randhreṇa**
**svānāṁ bhāva-saroruham**
**dhunoti śamalaṁ kṛṣṇaḥ**
**salilasya yathā śarat**

When Krishna enters the heart through the ear, He captures the lotus of the heart and then gradually makes all the dirt in the heart disappear. Just as when the autumn season comes, all the water everywhere becomes pure, so also, when Krishna enters our hearts, all the impurities within will gradually vanish, and only Krishna will remain forever.

# The Hare Krishna Mantra

Before chanting the holy name of Krishna, we must first chant the Pañcha-tattva *mantra:*

**śrī kṛṣṇa chaitanya prabhu nityānanda**
**śrī advaita gadādhara śrīvāsādi gaura-bhakta-vṛnda**

The Pañcha-tattva, or five features of the Absolute Truth, came to give the Hare Krishna *mahā-mantra* to the fallen devotees of this age, so they are the general representation of *guru* for us. They help us to enter into the domain of Krishna and also the plane of Śrī Chaitanya Mahāprabhu.

After chanting the Pañcha-tattva *mantra,* we should count on the beads of the *japa-mālā* and chant the *mahā-mantra:*

**Hare Krishna Hare Krishna Krishna Krishna Hare Hare**
**Hare Rāma Hare Rāma Rāma Rāma Hare Hare**

While counting beads and chanting the holy name, the beads should be placed inside a cloth bag, and the

Śrī Chaitanya Mahāprabhu and associates ecstatically chanting the Hare Krishna *mahā-mantra*.

index finger, which is generally considered inauspicious, should not touch the beads, but should remain outside the bag. Generally we use the thumb and middle finger to count. One should chant sixteen rounds, as recommended by Bhaktivedanta Swāmī Mahārāj, but if there is any emergency, he must chant at least four rounds; the *mālā* should not be kept fasting.

In the process of counting, we begin from the bigger beads and go towards the smaller, and again return in the same line. The giant bead in the center is called Mount Sumeru. We must not cross over that.

This *harināma mahā-mantra* is found in the *Upaniṣads*, as well as in the *Agni Purāṇa* and the *Brahmāṇḍa Purāṇa*. In the *Kalisantaraṇa Upaniṣad*, it is recommended as the highest *mantra*, and scholars have mentioned this *mantra* as a means of address only; no appeal should be attached to that. This Hare Krishna *mahā-mantra* is the *yuga dharma nāma*, or the process of God realization especially meant for the present age, *Kali-yuga*. We find the *mahā-mantra* mentioned everywhere in the *Purāṇas*. This *mantra* can be chanted silently, mentally, and aloud. It has been given to us by Mahāprabhu as the general recommendation for the fallen souls. He has given it for all, whether they are qualified or unqualified. The only condition for receiving it is *śraddhā*, faith.

It is mentioned in the *Padma Purāṇa* that there are ten kinds of offenses we must try to avoid in the chanting of the Hare Krishna *mahā-mantra*. There are also four kinds of *nāmābhāsa*, or apathetic chanting, which will not give us entrance into the domain of mercy. Mere liberation will be effected by that kind of invocation.

These two improper kinds of chanting stem from our tendencies for exploitation and renunciation. We must chant the name with the spirit of service and avoid the ten offenses.

### ABUSING SAINTS

**The first offense** is to abuse the devotees who are the agents of spreading the greatness and nobility of the Supreme Lord, Krishna. If we abuse and dishonor His agents, then the name is dissatisfied. Only the devotees of Krishna are real saints, because they are after eternal life. Those persons who worship demigods for temporary gain are not considered saints. They may be neglected, for they are not devotees. Saint means Vaiṣṇava, or devotee. All others, such as the worshipers of demigods, are not considered saints. We avoid them. A saint is one who has no ambition in his life but to have a connection of loving service with the Supreme Lord. Only those who are agents of eternal truth, absolute good, are to be considered saintly. We should not abuse such saintly persons.

### DEMIGOD WORSHIP

**The second offense** concerns how we should treat the demigods, including Śiva, Śakti, the Sun-god, and others. They are not to be considered equal to or greater than Viṣṇu, or Krishna. They are under Him, and they are all inferior to Him. They are given engagements by the Supreme Lord, Krishna, and they have to discharge their duties according to His order. They are never equal or superior to Krishna.

## GURU: GOOD AS GOD

**The third offense** is to consider the *guru* a human being. Although so many human symptoms may be found in him, still, according to our sincerity to meet Godhead, the Lord descends and represents Himself in the *guru* to satisfy our hunger for the truth. We must see him as the agent of the Lord. It has been advised to us in a general way not to think of the *guru* as a mortal being, because if our attempt to attain the Absolute is sincere, then He will also come to us to deliver us. God is omniscient, so through a particular agent who acts as His representative, He comes here to accept us and take us up to the higher plane. We are ordered by the advice of the scriptures to see the *guru* as the representative of the Absolute, because none can give us Krishna but He Himself.

God's presence should be perceived in our *gurudeva*. We should see that God has come to give Himself to us. Generally we find mortal signs in the body of the spiritual master, but we must transcend that. The Ganges water may be filthy in external appearance, but still the dirty Ganges water can purify us by its touch. To our material senses the Deity seems to be wood, stone, or earth, but that is our polluted vision. Krishna is there, and sometimes He is seen to walk and to talk with devotees of a higher

His Divine Grace Śrīla Śrīdhar Mahārāj chanting the Hare Krishna *mantra* softly on the *tulasī* beads of the *japa-mālā*.

order. We must not think that He is made of material stuff. When we go and stand before the Deity, we should not think that we can see Him, but that He is seeing us. He is in the subjective plane; I am His object.

He is mercifully seeing us to purify us. In this way our vision must be adjusted. Krishna was killed by a hunter; the atheists will interpret that it was an ordinary incident, but it is not so. Sītā was stolen by Rāvaṇa. This is all external, all illusory. The real truth is above, in the transcendental realm. So, we are requested by the expert transcendentalists and by the *śāstra* to see that our *gurudeva* is above these mortal signs. Krishna says:

**ācāryaṁ māṁ vijānīyān**
**nāvanmanyeta karhicit**
**na martya-buddhyāsūyeta**
**sarva-deva-mayo guruḥ**

"I Myself am the *āchārya*. Do not think that the *guru* is an ordinary man. I myself reside within the heart of *gurudeva* with all My parts and parcels, for the benefit of the disciple."

## BLASPHEMING THE SCRIPTURES

**The fourth offense** is *śāstra nindā:* blaspheming the *śāstra*, the scriptures. Of course this means those scriptures which are concerned with praising the greatness and nobility of Krishna, not others. We must not abuse those scriptures that instruct us about God and His devotees, and teach us the eternal good.

## HOLY NAME: GOD IN SOUND

**The fifth offense** is to interpret the holy name of Krishna with the help of the dictionary and grammar, to find diverse meanings in the words of the name. The sound is transcendental. The dictionary, grammar, and any other books of mundane knowledge cannot limit or qualify the holy name. Above the material sound of the name is the transcendental sound within (*śabda-brahma*). The name itself is the Supreme Person incarnate by His own free will. He is inseparable from His name and fully present in His sound form.

The *vaikuṇṭha śabda*, transcendental sound, is different from the mundane sound that can be produced by the tongue and lips. In homeopathic medicine, all the globules are apparently the same, but the potency within is all-important. It is something like that. The ordinary sound of the name, and the sound vibrated by a pure devotee come from different planes. The difference is in the potency within. The holy name descends from the spiritual world and comes to express itself by dancing on the tongue. The transcendental sound of the holy name is inseparably connected with the person whom it represents.

**The sixth offense** is to consider the glories of the holy name of Krishna to be a concoction.

## To Sin and Chant is Suicidal

**The seventh offense** is to sin on the strength of the holy name. The scriptures declare that one name is sufficient to clear all the sins one can commit, so if we go on indulging, committing many sins with the idea that we will chant one name to cleanse the sin, it will be an offense to the name, and not the name proper. We cannot try to utilize Him for our service; He is above all this *māyā*. The real name will not appear there. We must not think, "I can do anything and everything, and the name will purify me." It is written in the scriptures that if you go on with this spirit it will be suicidal.

### HARE KRISHNA: THE SUPREME PURIFICATION

**The eighth offense** is to think that chanting the holy name is another pious activity like penance, pilgrimage, giving in charity, service to the country, and so on. If we think lightly of the holy name in this way, then we commit an offense, because the holy name is absolute and these other processes have only a partial, relative position. Other processes are partial; they award some success in this mundane world, but the name can give the Lord Himself. So, no other process of purification can hold the same position as chanting the holy name of Krishna. It is supreme and none can come close to it.

### FORBIDDEN FOR THE FAITHLESS

**The ninth offense** is to give the name to those who do not deserve it, who have no faith in chanting the name. If you press them to chant the holy name, a bad reaction will come to you. Also, without getting any inspiration, we should not make disciples and give *harināma* initiation. We will commit offense against the name if we make a business or trade with name-giving. If we give the name to anyone and everyone, out of greed for becoming a *guru*, then it will be an offense. Without sanction from above, if one runs to become a *guru* to get name and fame with some mundane purpose, then it is a great offense.

## BACK TO GODHEAD

**The tenth offense** is to be too much addicted to a particular thing, or to have too much affinity towards the body and bodily wealth. When a boat is anchored, rowing will simply move the boat around the anchor. The anchor must be taken up, and then the boat can move forward. So, we must not anchor ourselves down with a particular thing. We must be open. The name will create some transformation within the mental system, and we must be open and unprejudiced enough to go where the name will send us. If we carefully try to avoid that transformation and stick to our present life, that is an offense against the name: to invite Him, and then ignore Him.

We must not accept the name as a foreign thing: He is our friend. We should be quite at home with Him. We are going to attain a very soothing and friendly connection by the realization of the holy name of Krishna, which is all-good, all-beautiful, and all-charming. By chanting the holy name we will attain our most desirable end of life and go back to God, back to home, and not to any foreign country.

We must take the name in a friendly, affectionate way. The name is the only object of our love. He is our friend, and not any anti-party. So, the name will take us home — not to any foreign land. That is our sweet home, and He is our sweet guardian. With this spirit, we shall go on chanting the holy name of Krishna.

These are the ten offenses to be avoided in chanting the Hare Krishna *mahā-mantra*: Hare Krishna Hare Krishna Krishna Krishna Hare Hare, Hare Rāma Hare Rāma Rāma Rāma Hare Hare.

## NĀMĀBHĀSA: THE TWILIGHT NAME

In chanting the holy name, there are also four kinds of *nāmābhāsa*. *Nāmābhāsa* means a faint connection with the holy name. *Nāmābhāsa* is neither offense nor service mood, but between the two. Its basis is renunciation, but we must also cast away this indifference and become earnest for serving the name, who is our friend and master. *Nāmābhāsa* may be classified into four categories. The first is *sānketyaṁ*: chanting indirectly, to indicate something else, as in the case of Ajāmila.

Ajāmila was a *brāhmaṇa's* son. Somehow, he connected with a low-class woman and entered into a degraded life as a *dacoit*, drinking and doing many other nasty things. After many years, the time came for his death. As he lay in a coma, suddenly he saw three messengers with a horrible appearance come and put a rope around his neck and begin to drag him away. He was horrified.

Just before this, he had seen his son Nārāyaṇa playing nearby, so he sought the help of the child and called "Nārāyaṇa!" But in the course of calling his name, Ajāmila thought within himself, "What can this boy Nārāyaṇa do? How will he deal with these three furious figures? He is nothing." So, by the connection of the holy name of Nārāyaṇa, Lord Nārāyaṇa came to his mind.

When in his apprehension his call for Lord Nārāyaṇa was sincere, four agents from Vaikuṇṭha descended. They were sober and mild, and addressed the Yamadūtas, the messengers of death saying:

"Who are you? Why have you come?"

"We have come because it is the last day of Ajāmila. He was a great sinner, and we have been sent by our king, Yamarāj, the Lord of death, to drag him away for punishment."

"Don't you know what is *dharma*, duty?"

"Oh yes, we know."

"Then why are you here?"

"He committed immense sin."

"Didn't you hear him take the name of Nārāyaṇa?"

"Yes we have heard. What of that? His whole life he has committed so many sinful acts, and only one name of Nārāyaṇa will do away with that? It is not possible."

"Oh, you have not been properly directed by your master. Now that Ajāmila has taken the name of Nārāyaṇa, his jurisdiction has at once changed. He is no longer under the jurisdiction of your master. Has he not given such instructions to you?"

"No, no, we do not know all these things."

"Then, go back, and ask him."

Ajāmila was released. Frightened by the posture and grandeur of the messengers of Viṣṇu, the Yamadūtas fled. Ajāmila thought, "What is the instruction to be learned here?"

This is *nāmābhāsa*. It is a faint connection with the holy name. It was neither out of faith, nor by the order of his *guru*, that he chanted the name of Nārāyaṇa. It was not that he purposely went to take the name, but by accident it flashed in his mind. Still, as a result of his previous pious activity, *nāmābhāsa* gave him salvation.

Ajāmila at once awoke; he remembered all his past sinful activities and began to repent. He began his journey towards Hardwar without speaking a single word to family or friend. There, he chanted the name of Nārāyaṇa for a long time. At the proper time, those four Viṣṇudūtas descended with a divine chariot and took him to the conscious spiritual domain of Vaikuṇṭha.

## TO JOKE AND CHANT

*Pārihāsya is* another kind of *nāmābhāsa*. *Pārihāsya* means jokingly. Sometimes in sport we may say, "Oh, you are chanting the name of Krishna?" If one is cutting jokes, ridiculing the Hare Krishna devotees in the street, and says "Hare Krishna," that may be *nāmābhāsa* if it is connected with his previous pious credits. *Mukti*, or liberation, may be effected by that kind of chanting, but not the opportunity for divine service.

## KRISHNA AS CODE NAME

Another form of *nāmābhāsa is stobha*: to use the name with some other intention. Sometimes these words, Nārāyaṇa, or Krishna may be used for some technical meaning, or for a code word. Jīva Goswāmī has taken advantage of this in his book of Sanskrit grammar, the *Harināmāmṛta-vyākaraṇa*. When one is playing the *mṛdaṅga* drum, using the names *gaura nitāi*, *gaura nitāi* to represent different drumbeats, it may be *nāmābhāsa*.

## INDIRECT CHANTING

*Helā* is another kind of *nāmābhāsa:* neglectfully chanting the name. When we are rising from bed in the morning sometimes, we may negligently say "Hare Krishna." In this way we may cast off our indolence. Even there it may be *nāmābhāsa*. It may liberate us from our present position, but may not give us entrance into Vaikuṇṭha. That is possible only through devotional service.

One Mohammedan, who was being killed by the tusk of a boar, shouted "*Haram!*" meaning, "This is abominable!" but because of his previous *sukṛti*, or pious credits, it became *nāmābhāsa*, and he achieved liberation by chanting the name of Lord Rāma.

*Nāmābhāsa* may come, and *mukti*, liberation, may be effected, but we cannot get the opportunity of service there. Only if our mind is surcharged with a serving attitude will it elevate us to the subtle and higher plane, otherwise not. If the tendencies for renunciation and exploitation are mixed with our chanting, it won't yield the desired result.

The chanting must be done with a service attitude (*sevonmukhe hi jihvādau*). What is our aim? We want the service of the Lord: "Die to live." We want a life of purity which is full of self-giving; we want a generous life. We want to live the life of those who want not to extract, but to give. We want a civilized life in the domain of higher civilization, where everyone is a giving unit, an emanating unit, and not an absorbing unit. There, everyone is especially God-centered and harmonious. They are all of the nature of divinity. And divinity means dedication towards the center of all harmony, the absolute good. So with that spirit, we are to chant the holy name, and every action should be done with devotion for Krishna. We should try to take the positive line of serving Viṣṇu and Vaiṣṇava, Krishna and His devotees, and with this sort of attitude we should chant the holy name of Krishna.

# Service of the Holy Name

**Student:** I have one question about chanting the Hare Krishna *mantra* on beads *(japa-mālā)*. My spiritual master has given me many preaching duties, so sometimes when I am trying to concentrate on my *japa-mālā*, instead of hearing the holy name, I think of all these different duties I have to do.

**Śrīdhar Mahārāj:** Śrīla Bhaktisiddhānta Saraswatī Ṭhākur emphasized that *kīrtan* means not only loudly singing the holy name, but preaching. Jīva Goswāmī has given a definition of *saṅkīrtan: bahubhir militvā yat kīrtanaṁ tad eva saṅkīrtanam:* "When many people come together and glorify the Supreme Lord, Krishna, it is known as *saṅkīrtan*." Śrī Chaitanya Mahāprabhu came and introduced *saṅkīrtan*. In this age of Kali, if the holy name is chanted congregationally, the combined efforts will be fruitful *(saṅgo śakti kalau yuge)*. There is the difference between the preaching mission of Śrīla Bhaktisiddhānta Saraswatī Ṭhākur, and the so-called *bhajana* of the *sahajiyās*, or imitationists.

Once, one of our Godbrothers was the subject of our *guru mahārāj's* stern remark. He was a man of good character, but his tendency was generally towards *nāma bhajana*. He did not like to do any other service, but was only inclined to chant the name of Krishna on his beads. I was in charge of the Delhi temple at the time, and was intimate with him, so I wrote to Prabhupāda: "If you permit, I would like to engage my Godbrother in some preaching work here in the Delhi temple." The letter that Prabhupād wrote is still here. He wrote me in his letter, "If you can bring him there and make him help you in the work of preaching, then you will be doing the service of a real friend to him. I don't recognize that sitting in the jungle of Balihati only chanting, counting beads, is *Kṛṣṇānuśīlanam*, the proper cultivation of Krishna consciousness."

## PREACHING MEANS A FIGHT

So, *kīrtan* means preaching, *śravaṇam*, *kīrtanam*. *Kīrtan* does not simply mean loudly chanting, but preaching. And preaching means there must be a fight with the opposition party. *Kīrtan* means a fight. *Kīrtan* creates the divine vibration which will fight with all the ordinary vibrations that are floating in this world in subtle and gross waves. So, Prabhupād told us that our *tulasī* beads should not fast. His minimum advice was that we must do some service in the form of chanting Hare Krishna while counting on beads, at least once daily. His exact words were, *mālikā upabāsa nā*: "The beads should not fast." And his general instruction was to preach as much as possible.

Once I had a talk with one of the big spiritual leaders of the Udipi temple in Madras. He told me, "Sometimes I preach about Madhvāchārya and the *bhakti* cult, but I have no time for *sādhana*, (regulated spiritual practices such as *japa*, *gayātrī mantra*, scriptural study, and so on). I supported him. Our *guru mahārāj* said that *hari-kathā*, preaching about Krishna, is no less important than *sādhana*. Rather, it is a more living thing. Preaching is more vital. When we are preaching, automatically we must have the maximum concentration. On the other hand, while chanting on our *japa* beads, we may be absentminded. When we are speaking about Krishna to another person, we must be all-attentive. Otherwise we cannot speak accurately. All our attention will automatically be concentrated when we talk about Krishna. And in writing about Krishna, accuracy is even more necessary than in speaking about Krishna. So, writing is also *kīrtan*. The cultivation of Krishna consciousness may even be more intense when we are engaged in writing about Krishna.

## GAUḌĪYA MAṬH: WAR AGAINST MĀYĀ

So, the preaching mission of Śrīla Bhaktisiddhānta Saraswatī Ṭhākur, the Gauḍiya Maṭh, has declared totalitarian war against *māyā*, illusion, and even all

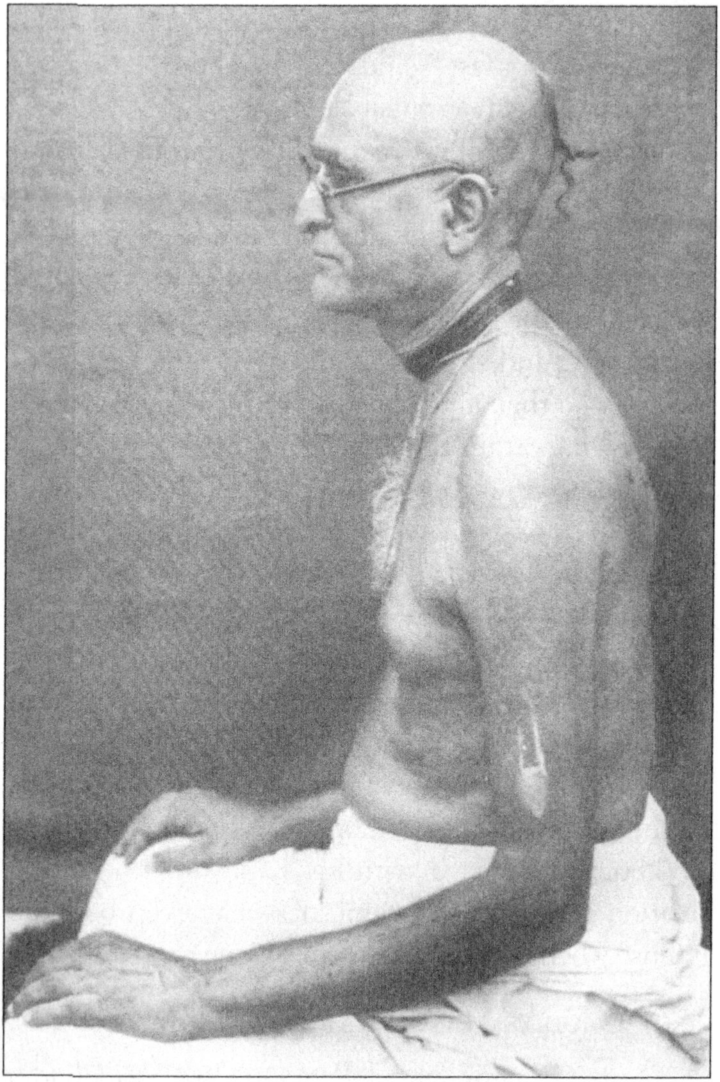

Śrīla Bhaktisiddhānta Saraswatī Ṭhākur, Founder-Āchārya of Śrī Gauḍīya Maṭh, declared totalitarian war against *māyā*, illusion, and even all other existing conceptions of religion.

other existing conceptions of religion. And our authority is *Śrīmad-Bhāgavatam* and Śrī Chaitanya Mahāprabhu. Divine love is the supreme most goal of every soul. Beauty and love is the *summum bonum*, our highest attainment; that is the ultimate controlling principle, and not power. And beauty and love are found at their highest position in Krishna in Vṛndāvana. The ultimate conception of the Absolute Truth is that of reality the beautiful and divine love. At the same time, the difference between lust and love should be clearly realized. That should not be misconceived. The acme of dedication is demonstrated in the love of the inhabitants of Vraja.

So, preaching *(saṅkīrtan)*, and not counting beads *(japa)*, is the real service of Krishna. But because we have taken a vow, and it is ordered by Mahāprabhu and our *gurudeva*, we must chant the holy name while counting beads; it is our duty. Our *guru mahārāj* told us, "The *japa* beads must not fast." So, if we engage ourselves in preaching work, there should be no doubt that we are really obeying the order of Mahāprabhu. Although he has advised us to chant one hundred thousand names, or sixty-four rounds daily, that is a provincial saying. What is really all-important is the spirit of service. We are not told that the *gopīs* always count the name on *tulasī* beads, yet they possess the highest position in the service of Krishna in Vṛndāvana.

## Vṛndāvan Express Train

So, Krishna *nāma* will help us greatly to go towards Vṛndāvana. Its importance is there. Like an express train, the holy naṃe of Krishna carries us to the goal without stopping at any other station. If we are chanting the name without any formal petition, without asking, "Give me this, give me that," it acts like a special train that will go to Vṛndāvana non-stop. There, the impurities of *karma* and *jñāna* are absent. The devotees of Vṛndāvana simply think, "I want Krishna. I do not know what is good or bad. I simply want Krishna."

**Student:** How many rounds did your *guru mahārāj* ask his initiated disciples to chant each day? Did he prescribe any set number?

**Śrīdhar Mahārāj:** His general recommendation was to chant twenty-five thousand names, sixteen rounds, daily, or at least four rounds minimum. When someone had no work, he could chant one hundred thousand names, or sixty-four rounds.

**Student:** Would Bhaktisiddhānta Saraswatī Ṭhākur give *harinām* initiation to someone who could only chant four rounds daily?

## Quality Not Quantity

**Śrīdhar Mahārāj:** There was no such consideration. Formally, one had to do some counting, but there was no rigid limitation. What he wanted from us was intense engagement in the service of the Lord, under the guidance of a Vaiṣṇava, because the all-important point is service. Our attainment of the goal is not insured simply by increasing the number of times we repeat the name; only by increasing the quality will we reach success.

There are so many sayings in the scriptures to encourage our realization of the holy name in different ways, but Śrīla Rūpa Goswāmī has given us a central thought. He quotes the *Padma Purāṇa*: *ataḥ śrī kṛṣṇa nāmādi na bhaved grāhyam indriyaiḥ*. Our senses, physical or mental, are ineligible to come in touch with the transcendental. The name is nonmaterial *(aprākṛta)*, without mundane limitation *(vaikuṇṭha)*. It belongs to another plane. So, nothing about Krishna—His name, form, qualities, or pastimes—can be touched by our physical or mental senses. But when we have a serving attitude, He comes down to us of His own accord. Only then can our tongue really pronounce the name of Krishna. Otherwise, only the physical sound of the letters of the name can be produced. Our tongue, our hands, physical sound, all these mundane things cannot come in touch with Krishna. Some intervening medium is necessary to connect this body with the supramundane. And that connection is our earnest desire to serve Krishna, to satisfy Him. A bulb won't light if there is no electricity. Only when the electrical current is there will the bulb be illumined. So, the name may appear on the tongue and in the ear, in the mind, or in writing, but we must have the connection from Vaikuṇṭha to this mundane world. And that connection is devotional service, a functional serving attitude. That alone can connect the physical realm with Vaikuṇṭha and Vṛndāvana.

## FIRING BLANK MANTRAS

Krishna will appear of His own accord. He will descend upon your tongue, and then your tongue will be able to chant the name of Krishna. A gun that has no bullet, but only a blank, may make some sound, but no bullet is actually fired. Similarly, chanting the name of Krishna without an attitude of service produces sound, but that is only tongue deep. It is like firing a gun with blanks instead of bullets. Our chanting of the holy name of Krishna must be surcharged with a serving temperament, the tendency to satisfy Krishna.

Otherwise the sound we produce is bogus. It is only an imitation, or a permutation. The holy name cannot be experienced by our senses. It is supramental and transcendental. An ordinary sound of this mundane world cannot be the name of Krishna. Our ear cannot even hear the name if that mediator, the serving attitude, is not there. The earnestness to satisfy Krishna's will must mediate between Krishna and the ear, through the mind. Then only will Krishna's name enter our ear and reveal to us His form, qualities, and pastimes. The holy name is not physical, it is *aprākṛta*, transcendental, supramundane. Only through our service attitude will it come down to this mundane world.

Our *guru mahārāj* laid the highest stress on developing a serving attitude. Otherwise it is all bogus, all imitation. And people will say, "Oh, there is no Krishna there. These men are hypocrites. They are only dancing and making noise, they are not surcharged with a serving spirit." Only through service can we directly come in contact with Krishna. The real point is to practice how to attain the spirit of service, Vaiṣṇava *seva*. The Vaiṣṇava is doing service, and we must imbibe from him the methods of attaining this serving attitude.

Under the order of a devotee we must practice to give ourselves. Self-abnegation and self-dedication are necessary. And that positive thing we will receive from a devotee. If children are given pen and paper in the beginning, it will not be fruitful, so a stone is given, and on the earth they practice writing. So, in the beginning, we must try to practice how we can develop a serving attitude, dedicating habit. It is our innate wealth, and that is our solace.

If we try to develop a serving attitude, the pure devotee will help us. It is said that if one is miserly, he should at least give some trash in charity to anyone. One says to a miser, "At least give some ash to others and let your hand practice giving." So, the serving spirit is a high thing. We must practice to give ourselves in the service of Krishna.

We must not be afraid that we are not attaining the highest form of service in *nāmabhajan*, the worship of the holy name. We should not think, "Why have I been asked to sweep the temple? Any ordinary man can do this." We must not be afraid of that. It is necessary for us to acquire a service attitude. Self-giving, selflessness, and self-forgetfulness are required. It is said that Socrates is an example of self-forgetfulness and Jesus Christ is an example of self-sacrifice. And for what purpose? For the cause of the Supreme. And for that we must have a positive connection with a devotee. Under his order we will connect with the plane of service. Our energy may go to the transcendental plane only by his grace or mediation. So, our *guru mahārāj*, Śrīla Bhaktisiddhānta Saraswatī Ṭhākur, laid ninety percent stress on developing a service attitude for preaching, and that should be our aim, whatever our position may be.

# Nectar of the Holy Name

Not only the sound of the holy name of Krishna is necessary, but also the proper meaning, the substance, the spirit of the sound. Only the physical aspect of the holy name is represented in *nāma-aparādha*, offensive chanting, not the real name. The real name is all spiritual. *Nāmākṣara bāhirāya baṭe tabhu nāma kabhu naya*: the sound of the letters of the name alone is never the real name. This is explained in the *Prema-vivarta* of Jagadānanda Paṇḍita, a book which is full of the philosophical conclusions of Krishna consciousness. It was published and edited by Bhaktivinoda Ṭhākur. There you will find this passage: *Nāmākṣara bāhirāya baṭe tabhu nāma kabhu naya*: merely the sound of the holy name of Krishna should never be thought of as the actual name.

Even in *nāmābhāsa*, the twilight dawning of the holy name which occurs before pure offenseless chanting, the sound of the name is there, but the inner substance of the name is not there. *Nāmābhāsa* can give us *mukti*, or emancipation from the negative side, the material world. But there we cannot trace participation in the positive side, the spiritual world. The name is absent there. The holy name of Krishna is a positive thing, and if we really want a touch of the holy name, we must gain admission into the positive world. When we are in the negative side, how can we get the touch of the name? *Nāmābhāsa* may give us liberation, but not participation in the devotional realm. So, the real name is not to be found in *nāmābhāsa* either.

## JEWELS OF THE VEDAS

Only a particular group of liberated souls worship the holy name, not everyone. Śrīla Rūpa Goswāmī has written in his *Nāmāṣṭakam* (1):

**nikhila-śruti-mauli-ratna-mālā-**
**dyuti-nīrājita-pāda-paṅkajānta**
**ayi mukta-kulair upāsyamānaṁ**
**paritas tvāṁ hari-nāma saṁśrayāmi**

"O Holy Name! The tips of the toes of Your lotus feet are eternally worshiped by the glowing effulgence radiating from the gemmed chapters of the *Upaniṣads*, the crest jewels of the *Vedas*. You are eternally adored and chanted by great liberated souls like Nārada and Śukadeva Goswāmī. O *hari nāma*! Clearing myself of all offenses, I take complete shelter of You."

Rūpa Goswāmī says that so many liberated souls worship the holy name of Krishna, offering their respects

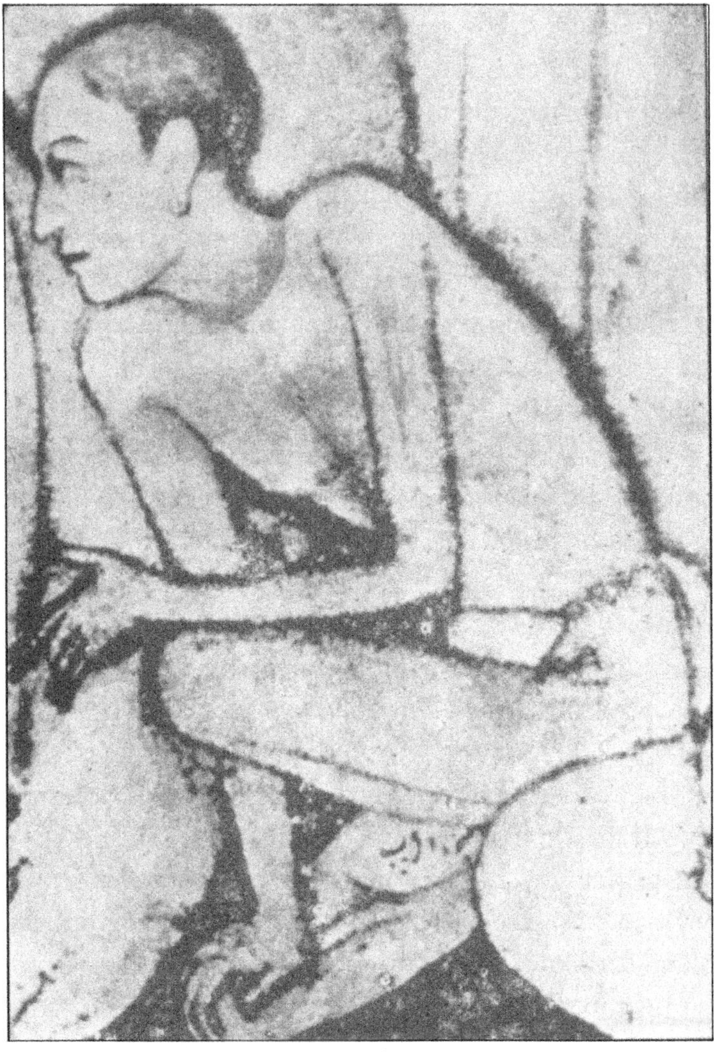

A sixteenth century portrait of Śrīla Rūpa Goswāmī. He was described in *Chaitanya-charitāmṛta* as, "an exact replica of Śrī Chaitanya Mahāprabhu." Śrīla Rūpa Goswāmī authored one hundred thousand verses on Mahāprabhu's instructions.

from all sides. He explains that the greatness of the holy name may not be found in the ordinary scriptures, but if you study all of them as a whole, you will find the very spirit of the holy name. Ordinary people may not find this in their study, but there are those who can collect the real substance, the real purpose from those vast writings, and detect the greatness of the holy name as the whole purpose of all the main Vedic scriptures.

## JUNGLE OF SOUNDS

The principle codes in the *śruti*, the *Vedas*, are giving hints about the holy name of Krishna. *Śruti* means *śabda*: that which can be grasped by the ear, the sound form of the revealed truth which has descended from above. The *Vedas* naturally tell us that we can approach the supreme reality only through sound. Otherwise they would be suicidal. If they do not say that by sound only we will attain the truth, then what is the necessity of the *Vedas* which are only embodied sounds? So, if we can trace their real characteristic we shall find that the principle *Vedas* say that by the cultivation of sound we can attain the Lord. So, we can come to understand this only through sound *(śabda pramāṇam)*. Sound alone can deliver reality. The *Vedas* must say so, otherwise they will only be an ineffective jungle of sounds.

*Śruti* means that which can be received through the ear, and that sound is absolute. The *śrutis* have come to declare to us that through sound alone we can attain the highest end. The main codes *(sūtras)* of the

"Just as while performing *āratī* we offer a lamp to show the Deity form of the Lord . . . the principle *śrutis* are helping us to have this clear conception: by sound only can we have the Supreme Lord."

*śruti* inform us: *nikhila-śruti-mauli-ratna-mālā*. *Mauli* means the principle scriptures. They are like so many gems or jewels forming a necklace. By their luster, the lotus feet of the holy name are being revealed. Just as while performing *ārati*, we offer a lamp to show the Deity form of the Lord more clearly to the ordinary people, the principle *śrutis* are helping us to have this perception; by sound only we can have the Supreme Lord.

Rūpa Goswāmī says that if we are more attentive to their meaning, we will find that the principle *śrutis* are only trying to show us the lotus feet of the holy name, just as during *ārati* the ghee lamp helps us to see the figure of the Lord. We may have a general view of the Deity, but with the help of the lamp, we can have a particular conception of the different parts of the body of the Lord. Similarly, we find that the principle *śrutis* with their light are trying to show us the lower portion of the holy name of Krishna. They are leading us and helping us to have a conception of the remotest part of the holy name, a vague conception that the name is everything. Rūpa Goswāmī says that those who are really liberated are all surrounding the holy name and offering praise and adoration. And he prays, "In this spirit, I take refuge in the holy name of Krishna."

The real meaning of the *Vedas is* difficult to understand. Some people will say, "Chanting Hare Krishna is not recommended in the *Vedas*. Rather, sometimes 'Krishna' is mentioned as the name of a demon. Why should we chant the name of Krishna?" In the *Vedas* (*Chāndogya Upaniṣad* 8.13.1), we find this verse:

**śyāmāc chavalaṁ prapadye**
**śavalāc chyāmaṁ prapadye**

"By the help of black *(śyāma)*, we shall be introduced to the service of white *(śavalā)*; by the help of white *(śavalā)*, we shall be introduced to the service of black *(śyāma)*." What is the meaning of this verse? Our *āchāryas* have explained that the absolute can be understood by the help of the energy and the energetic. *Śyāma* means Krishna, who is blackish, and *śavalā*, white, means Rādhārāṇī. So, by the help of Rādhā, we can have the service of Krishna, and by the help of Krishna, we can have the service of Rādhārāṇī.

## GOD THROUGH SOUND

So, Rūpa Goswāmī says that only a superficial study of the *Vedas* will frustrate us. But if we search with a positive mind, by the grace of the *sādhus*, the *āchāryas*, and the *mahājanas* we will find that the principle *śrutis* are leading us towards the conception that the whole object of all the Vedic sounds is that central sound; the holy name of Krishna. There are so many sections of the *Vedas* that have come to distribute the tidings of the absolute realm, but there must be a center. So, the principle sounds are all emitting light like a torch, to show us that they have a central sound which represents the supreme whole, and that is Krishna. So many liberated souls are all around, offering their respects to the name of Krishna, that central sound from which all Vedic *mantras* have come to give us some idea of the sound aspect of the absolute center. This is Rūpa Goswāmī's argument.

The branches of the *Vedas* are all sounds, and so many sounds must come from a central position. They cannot but direct one who has a proper eye towards that fountainhead of sound, saying, "Go! Run towards that direction! In our source you will find everything. We are all partially representing so many things but we have a center, we have a fountainhead. Go in that direction and you will find the sound that can sufficiently satisfy you, and you may also be introduced to other aspects of that sound."

The holy name of Krishna is most important; it is no less than Krishna Himself. It fully represents the whole. Rūpa Goswāmī says, "O Holy Name, I take refuge under Your lotus feet. You are the grand, central sound who has given cohesion to all the sounds in the revealed scriptures."

And Sanātan Goswāmī, who is the spiritual master of Rūpa Goswāmī, says:

> **jayati jayati nāmānanda-rūpaṁ murārer**
> **viramita-nija-dharma-dhyāna-pūjādi-yatnam**
> **katham api sakṛd-āttaṁ muktidaṁ prāṇīnāṁ yat**
> **paramam amṛtam ekaṁ jīvanaṁ bhūṣaṇaṁ me**

"Let ecstasy in the service of the divine name be victorious. If somehow we can come in contact with that sound, *nāma rūpaṁ murāreḥ*, then all our other activities will be paralyzed; we will have no necessity of performing any other activity. Our many variegated duties will have no importance to us at all if we can achieve the service of the divine name of Krishna."

*Dharma* means the business engagement of the *karmis* or fruitive workers. *Dhyāna* means retiring from this physical world and performing meditation from within, trying to exploit the internal world. Both of these are stopped, paralyzed by the ecstasy of service to the divine name.

The Rāmānuja sect worships Lakṣmī-Nārāyaṇa in the mood of opulence and veneration in Vaikuṇṭha. By the ecstasy of the holy name, that will also be stopped. One who gets the real grace of the divine name of Krishna will retire from all phases of these different kinds of worship, namely *varṇāśrama dharma*, or social duty; *dhyāna*, the internal meditation of the *jñānis* (mental speculators) and *yogis*; and *puja*, the opulent worship of Vaikuṇṭha, after liberation, which attracts the followers of the Rāmānuja *sampradāya*. The holy name will take us to the perception of Goloka, Krishna's own abode, where we will have to completely retire from all these other phases of our divine life. We will have to retire from any work, even if it may be done for Krishna. We will have to give up internal meditation and calculation, and even *pūjā*, worship in awe and reverence.

The holy name will stop all these tendencies, and we will find so much sweetness in chanting the name that we won't be able to give attention to anything else. When we really come in contact with the sound aspect of the absolute, then all our other enthusiastic endeavors and functions will be paralyzed. We will be unable to attempt them. We will take to the name only. Then, when the name allows us to perform other services again, we will be able to do them. The name has such power, such a high degree of potency that it will stop all other branches of service, and charm you.

## "I WANT MILLIONS OF EARS!"

In the writings of Rūpa Goswāmī we find this verse:

**tuṇḍe tāṇḍavanī ratiṁ vitanute tuṇḍāvalī-labdhaye**
**karṇa-kroḍa kaḍambinī ghaṭayate karṇārbudebhyaḥ spṛhām**
**cetaḥ prāṅgaṇa-saṅginī vijayate sarvendriyāṇāṁ kṛtiṁ**
**no jāne janitā kiyadbhir amṛtaiḥ kṛṣṇeti varṇa-dvayī**

When the holy name of Krishna descends and captures the tongue and lips, it controls them so strongly that it engages them in chanting the holy name as if the lips and tongue have gone mad. In this way, the power of the name descends in them, and one feels that only one tongue and one mouth are not enough; thousands of mouths are necessary to taste the name. Then the holy name of Krishna enters the ear with such a great force and current that the ears are captured, and one thinks that only two ears are insufficient; he wants millions of ears to attend to the sweet current entering the ears. Two ears are nothing to him; he wants millions of ears. The nectar of the holy name is coming like a flood through his ears, pushing its way within the heart.

It is so sweet that as it goes to capture the heart, the center of all senses, everything is paralyzed. Wherever that sweet aggressor touches, the whole thing is captured with such intensity that everything else is ignored. Rūpa Goswāmī writes, "I don't know, I can't say, I fail to express how much nectar there is in the holy name of Krishna. These two syllables contain so much sweetness, and such a high quality of sweetness. And this sweetness is so aggressive that it captures everything." This verse is found in the *Vidagdha-Mādhava* written by Śrīla Rūpa Goswāmī.

In his book, *Śaraṇāgati*, Śrīla Bhaktivinoda Ṭhākur has explained the *Nāmāṣṭakam*, eight prayers in glorification of the holy name, written by Rūpa Goswāmī. The whole thing is described there very beautifully.

He writes, "My heart is just like a desert, hot with the rays of the sun. This is my internal mental condition. The desire for mortal things cannot satisfy me because by nature they are death-producing. And not one or two, but thousands of such death-producing desires have taken shelter in my mind. So, my subconscious region is always burning. This is my condition.

"But somehow, by the grace of the *sādhu* and *guru*, the holy name of Krishna with its infinite prospect has entered through the holes of my ears and reached the plane of my heart. And there, with some peculiar hope, with infinite, auspicious possibilities, it touched my heart with a new kind of nectar.

## ECSTASY OF THE NAME

"New hope is aroused by that sound. Then by force, it comes from the heart towards the tongue. Not that by the endeavor of my tongue I am producing that sound —no. What came from the heart of a saint through my ear, entered my heart, and that forcibly appeared upon my tongue, and began to dance. That is the holy name proper. It descends from above. It cannot be produced by the material form of this tongue. Its source is above.

"And through an agent of the absolute it comes through the ear to the heart. From the heart it gathers some sympathy, then the holy name of Krishna forcibly appears upon the tongue, and begins to dance. With great force it comes to the end of the tongue, and that sweet sound begins its dancing."

The real effects of the divine name have been described here. If it is a living and real name, the voice will be choked up, there will be shivering in the body, and the legs will be unable to stand. Sometimes tears will flow in a current on the body, and one's hairs will stand on end. Sometimes changes of color will be found in the body, and we will be unable to find any trace of the mind or consciousness. We may fall in a swoon, the whole body and mind will appear as if it is being attacked, shivering, and influenced in different ways. Apparently it may seem that so many troubles are created in the body and the mind, but the real heart is overflowing with a particular kind of strange, sweet juice.

## OCEAN OF NECTAR

Sometimes one thinks, "I am in an ocean of nectar. My whole existence is within an ocean of nectarine liquid. I am beside myself. I can't understand where I am. Where am I? What is this? What is all about me? It has almost made me mad. Am I a madman? Where is my past experience, my seriousness, my gravity, where are they? What am I?

"I have been converted wholesale by a foreign thing. I am a doll in the hands of a great force, which is also so affectionate to me. I can't ascertain how it is possible that by my faith I have entered this great, unknown environment, unexperienced before.

"And at last I find that I am captivated. My entire being, within and without, has been captured by a particular sweet force. I can't help being prey to such a sweet power. I can't give any proper description of this. I came to take shelter under Him and accept Him as my guardian; now at His hand I am being dealt with in such a merciless and despotic way. Still, I feel that everything is very pleasing, beyond my experience. What is this?

"I can't resist anymore. I am fully captured. Let my fate go anywhere. I can't come out. I am a captive in the hand of a sweet friend; my whole independence is gone. There is no way left to me but to surrender. I am unable to describe my real position. I find that He's an autocrat. Whatever He likes to do, He will do. Since it is not possible for me to give any resistance, I must surrender. Let me also cooperate with whatever He is pleased to do. Otherwise, what can I do? I am helpless.

"Sometimes I find that the sweetness of the name is condensed like a blossoming flower, and very wonderful streams of sweet current are flowing from it. The holy name contains so many sweet variegated forms of current within Him, and He is wonderfully expressing Himself in different ways. Sometimes He emanates a peculiar type of color and figure, and disappears.

"So many charming aspects are shown as if to my eyes within, and He forcibly takes me to surrender at the foot of that altar. He shows Himself in His full-fledged form, in Vṛndāvana, in His Vraja *līlā*, with Rādhārāṇī, and He takes me there. I find that I am in the midst of His peculiar, very sweet and loving paraphernalia. And He says, 'You see! I have so many wonderful things. This is your home. I am not merely imagination, but concrete reality. You will find here that the environment is very favorable and sweet. You are to live here.'

"I see there that he is dealing in different ways with His associates, in different *rasas*. And I find that I have another body that has emerged from my previous one, and that has a permanent place here in His service. Such a new life I find here. And then I find ultimately that all consideration of my past life and experience has vanished. And it is true: my real life is here. This is proper, and that was a sham, that life has vanished.

"Then I find that chanting the holy name gives me new encouragement, a new prospect, and new hope. Whatever we want, whatever is our internal demand, it is supplied by the name. If we take the name, all our internal hankerings will be fulfilled. It is eternal, it is the purest of the pure, and it is full of ecstasy. Now I find I have been completely converted.

"Now, my innermost hankering is this: let whatever is against this sweet name vanish eternally from the world. If anything is in opposition to this sweet life, let it vanish, and if necessary, I will give my life to make it disappear from the world forever. Then others will be able to enjoy it at their free will. No hindrance should come to that fulfillment of life. It has no other second. So, everyone may come here, and if necessary, I will sacrifice myself to finish any opposition, so that all can smoothly, peacefully, and without any danger, enjoy this absolute, sweet, and blissful life." This is the statement of Śrīla Bhaktivinoda Ṭhākur, in the final song of his book, *Śaraṇāgati (Surrender)*.

# Reality the Beautiful

Rāmānanda Rāya was a married man, but he was recognized by Śrī Chaitanya Mahāprabhu as a master of his senses to the extreme degree. Once a *brāhmaṇa* priest named Pradyumna Miśra came to Mahāprabhu and told Him, "I would like to hear about Krishna from Your lips." Mahāprabhu said, "I do not know anything about Krishna, but Rāmānanda Rāya knows. Go to him and hear about Krishna. Take My name, and perhaps he will talk with you."

Pradyumna Miśra was hesitant, but he went and observed Rāmānanda Rāya for some time and then returned and reported to Mahāprabhu. Mahāprabhu asked him, "Have you heard about Krishna from Rāmānanda?" "No." "Why?" "I saw him engaged in something objectionable. I watched for some time, and then returned here." "What did you see?" Pradyumna Miśra answered, "I saw Rāmānanda Rāya training some young dancing girls!"

Girls who are generally devoted to the service of the Jagannāth Deity from a young age are known as *deva-dāsīs*. They do not marry, and sometimes their character is not very good. Pradyumna Miśra saw Rāmānanda Rāya training *deva-dāsīs* in a very objectionable way. He was showing them how to go before the Jagannāth Deity and dance and sing. He showed them how their posture should be, how they should gesture, and how their looks should be enticing. And for such training he would sometimes even touch their private parts. So Pradyumna Miśra told Mahāprabhu, "Seeing Rāmānanda doing all these things, I had no regard for him, so for some time I saw him busily engaged in that matter, and then I went away."

## MASTER OF THE SENSES

Mahāprabhu told him, "Don't underestimate Rāmānanda Rāya. He is the master of his senses. There is not a tinge of craft in him. Even I feel trouble from sense disturbance within Me, but Rāmānanda has no such trouble. We have no direct experience that a stage can be attained where it is possible to be above mundane sense pleasure, but we have only heard through the scriptures that there is a stage when a man may transcend all these gross attachments.

"This is mentioned in the *Śrīmad-Bhāgavatam* (10.33.39):

> **vikrīḍitaṁ vraja-vadhūbhir idaṁ ca viṣṇoḥ**
> **śraddhānvito 'nuśṛṇuyād atha varṇayed yaḥ**
> **bhaktiṁ parāṁ bhagavati pratilabhya kāmaṁ**
> **hṛd-rogam āśv apahinoty acireṇa dhīraḥ**

"One who hears with firm faith the supramundane amorous affairs of Lord Krishna and the *gopīs*, as described by a pure devotee of the Lord, soon becomes freed from mundane lust and achieves divine love of Krishna.

"One may be engaged bodily in such activities, while his heart is elsewhere. And there is only one who is of that type, Rāmānanda Rāya. There are not big numbers of Rāmānandas; there is only one Rāmānanda, who has acquired such a stage because he is well-versed in the kind of sentiment and realization which is necessary for the service of Krishna and the *gopīs*. His heart is completely dedicated to the cause of Krishna; He has no selfish interest. He is always in Krishna consciousness, and whatever he does is for Krishna's satisfaction, so don't think ill of him. Go there again."

## MAD FOR KRISHNA

Then Pradyumna Miśra again went to see Rāmānanda Rāya, and Rāmānanda began their conversation by saying "Oh, on that day I could not oblige you. But again you have come to hear about Krishna. How fortunate I am!" In the morning, Rāmānanda Rāya began to speak, and when the afternoon came, still he was madly talking about Krishna. He completely forgot about eating, bathing, or anything else. He was mad, incessantly speaking of Krishna. Then, when it was late, his servants came twice, thrice, to ask him to take bath and eat his dinner, and finally, he had to leave the talk and go. Then Pradyumna Miśra returned to Mahāprabhu and said, "Yes, I have heard from Rāmānanda Rāya, and my heart is full from hearing about Krishna from him."

Mahāprabhu Himself had heard from Rāmānanda Rāya, and He said, "Rāmānanda knows what is Krishna. What I taught to Rūpa and Sanātana, I heard from Rāmānanda." It is mentioned that Mahāprabhu took *dīkṣā*, initiation, from Īśvara Purī; for preaching purposes he took *sannyāsa*, the renounced order, from Keśava Bhāratī; and for entrance into the transcendental pastimes of Krishna in Vṛndāvana, He took *rāga mārga* initiation from Rāmānanda Rāya. Of course, Īśvara Purī, Keśava Bhāratī, and Rāmānanda Rāya never thought of themselves as the *guru* of Śrī Chaitanya Mahāprabhu. But it was seen that Mahāprabhu treated Rāmānanda with some respect. It is mentioned in the *Chaitanya-caritāmṛta (Madhya* 8.204*)* that if one wants to enter into the spontaneous devotion of Krishna's pastimes in Vraja, it is required that he take shelter of a confidential maidservant in conjugal mellow, *mādhurya rasa (sakhī vinā ei līlāya anyera nāhi gati)*.They are masters of that situation. The whole storehouse of this *mādhurya līlā* is in the hands of those maidservants. Only they can give it to others. In *mādhurya rasa*, the *guru is* seen in the form and spirit of a *sakhī*, a maidservant of Rādhārāṇī *(guru rūpa sakhī)*. Rāmānanda Rāya was Viśākhā-sakhī, the right-hand personal attendant of Śrīmatī Rādhārāṇī.

Śrī Chaitanya Mahāprabhu gives us a hint of the necessity of approaching a confidential associate of Śrīmatī Rādhārāṇī when He says to Rāmānanda:

**kibā vipra, kibā nyāsī, śūdra kene naya**
**yei kṛṣṇa-tattva vettā, sei 'guru' haya**

"Why do you shrink away from instructing Me? I am learning so much from you. You are well-versed in the affairs of Krishna, so you are *guru*; therefore I am hearing from you. Whoever is the master of that storehouse of *Krishna-līlā*, and whoever can distribute it—he is *guru*; of this, there is no doubt."

The famous talks between Rāmānanda Rāya and Śrī Chaitanya Mahāprabhu took place on the banks of the Godāvarī river. The name Godāvarī is significant, for it indicates that place where the highest fulfillment of our spiritual senses was given. The fullest engagement of all our senses was announced there on the banks of the Godāvarī: "Your senses are not to be rejected. If you can give up the spirit of exploitation and renunciation, then your senses will have their fulfillment with Krishna. Those tendencies bar your approach to Krishna. To properly approach Krishna, you will have to utilize your senses to the fullest extent." That was dealt with on the banks of the Godāvarī.

## THE ULTIMATE GOAL OF LIFE

There, in his famous conversations with Rāmānanda Rāya, Śrī Chaitanya Mahāprabhu began the approach

সখী বিনা এই লীলায় অন্যের নাহি গতি ।
সখীভাবে যে তাঁরে করে অনুগতি ॥ ২০৪ ॥
রাধাকৃষ্ণ-কুঞ্জসেবা-সাধ্য সেই পায় ।
সেই সাধ্য পাইতে আর নাহিক উপায় ॥ ২০৫ ॥

The original Bengali text of the conversation between Śrī Chaitanya Mahāprabhu and Rāmānanda Rāya, recorded in the *Chaitanya-charitāmṛta* five hundred years ago by Krishnadās Kavirāj Goswāmī.

to pure devotional service in a general and comprehensive way. This is recorded in the *Madhya-līlā* of *Chaitanya-caritāmṛta* (8.51-313). He asked Rāmānanda Rāya, *prabhu kahe*, "*paḍa śloka sādhyera nirṇaya*": "What is the ultimate goal of life? I not only want to hear your statements, but also evidence from the scriptures."

The answer came from Rāmānanda Rāya: *rāya kahe*, "*sva-dharmācaraṇe viṣṇu-bhakti haya.*" "Discharge your own duty, without expecting anything in return." *Sva dharma* means *varṇāśrama dharma*, Vedic social stratification. "You are posted in your present position by your previous *karma*. According to your present position, you have to discharge your duties on one condition: you must do them without remuneration. If you go on with your duties in *varṇāśrama dharma*, without any mundane aim, you can achieve *viṣṇu-bhakti*, devotion to God. This is confirmed in the *Viṣṇu Purāṇa* (3.8.9):

**varṇāśramācāra-vatā**
**puruṣeṇa paraḥ pumān**
**viṣṇur ārādhyate panthā**
**nānyat tat-toṣa-kāraṇam**

"The only way to please the Supreme Personality of Godhead, Lord Viṣṇu, is to worship Him by properly executing one's prescribed duties in the social system of *varṇa* and *āśrama*." Here, Rāmānanda Rāya says that *viṣṇu-bhakti*, adherence to the Lord who is permeating everything, is the object and ultimate destination of our life. This is the Vāsudeva conception: everything is in Him, and He is everywhere. Rāmānanda explained that from our local interests, we must come to embrace the general interest, and that must reach the level of Viṣṇu consciousness: *viṣṇu-bhakti*. Our submission to Viṣṇu, the internal spirit who is everywhere, is the object of life. We must connect with Him and live accordingly, not a phenomenal life, but a spiritual life pertaining to a deeper, more subtle plane.

## DEVOTION MIXED WITH DESIRES

Śrī Chaitanya Mahāprabhu said, "This is superficial; go deeper." Of course, it may be thought that actual theistic life begins from here, giving up the special, local purpose, and acting for a universal purpose, as already ordered and programmed in the *Vedas* and *Upaniṣads*. But Śrī Chaitanya Mahāprabhu said, "This is superficial; go deeper."

Then, Rāmānanda Rāya said, *kṛṣṇe karmārpaṇa—sarva-sādhya-sāra*: "To offer the results of one's activities to Krishna is the essence of all perfection." In *varṇāśrama dharma*, it is the fashion that people are generally engaged in external activities and do not care to give up the fruits of their action. Even if they do, they have no direct consciousness of Viṣṇu or Krishna. They worship the goddess Durgā, perform the *śrāddhā* funeral ceremony and execute so many other religious practices. Indirectly, it is ultimately connected with Viṣṇu. They may or may not know how, but the link is there. That is the general conception of *varṇāśrama*, but here, Rāmānanda says that it will be better to have direct consciousness that Krishna is the authority. All the results of whatever we do within the *varṇāśrama* social system must be given to Krishna. If we perform all our physical, social, national and spiritual activities in Krishna consciousness, then we can approach the fulfillment of our goal in life.

Śrī Chaitanya Mahāprabhu said "This is superficial; go deeper." Then Rāmānanda Rāya revealed new light, quoting the *Bhagavad-gītā* (18.66): *sarva-dharmān parityajya mām ekaṁ śaraṇaṁ vraja*, "Give up all your duties, and just surrender to Me." We must be particular with the object of life, not the external activities of *varṇāśrama*. Less importance should be given to the form of our activity; whether I am a king, a *brāhmaṇa* intellectual, or a worker does not matter. We may think, "I have this sort of duty, I have that sort of duty," but that does not matter very much. We must have no attachment for that. The king may leave his kingdom and take to a brahmanical life of renunciation and austerity. A *śūdra* may give up his labor, become a beggar, and chant the name of Krishna. A *brāhmaṇa* may give up his performance of sacrifice and become a mendicant. So, we are to be particular about the aim of life, not the form of our duty. We must exclusively devote ourselves to the cause of the Lord, ignoring our present paraphernalia and duty.

## KNOWLEDGE AND DEVOTION

Śrī Chaitanya Mahāprabhu said, "This is also superficial; go ahead—deeper." Then, Rāmānanda Rāya explained *jñāna-miśra bhakti*, devotional service mixed with knowledge, by quoting from the *Bhagavad-gītā* (18.54) where Krishna says:

**brahma-bhūtaḥ prasannātmā**
**na śocati na kāṅkṣati**
**samaḥ sarveṣu bhūteṣu**
**mad-bhaktiṁ labhate parām**

One who has come to the stage of identifying himself with spirit above matter has nothing to do with this mundane world. Any loss or gain in this mundane world is of no use to him. He is spirit; his prospect is in the world of soul, and he has nothing to do with this material world, whether it is laudable or blamable. He is already settled in the consciousness that he is soul proper and has nothing to do with matter, so within himself he feels satisfaction. He is *ātmārāma*: self-content; he neither mourns, nor aspires for anything. If something is lost, does he mourn? No. He thinks, "This is nothing; it is only matter." And when something is gained, he is not overly cheerful, because it is only matter; it is unnecessary and unimportant. Now true devotional service can begin. His soul can begin living in the spiritual plane, with a pure serving attitude, unmixed with any mundane aspiration. When one attains the spiritual platform, he gets the opportunity to practice a higher type of service.

Śrī Chaitanya Mahāprabhu said, "This is also superficial. Such a person is only on the verge of devotional service; he has no substantial touch of devotion. He has not entered the domain of *bhakti*; he is just waiting in the marginal position, at the door. He may attain *bhakti*, but he has not yet achieved it. His negative forces are finished, but still, he is just at the door; he has not yet entered. He may enter; he may not enter. From there, if he gets anything, it will be pure, but he is still at the door.

## BEYOND SPIRIT, "GO DEEPER"

Rāmānanda Rāya then said, *jñāne prayāsam udapāsya namanta eva*: "It is a very difficult thing to cross the charm of knowledge." We think, "I want to understand everything first, and then I shall act." Calculation and an underlying suspicion is there. Before we act, we want to know everything fully; only then will we risk our capital. The ego, the "I" is very strong, and he wants to have an account of his loss and gain. He thinks, "I am the master. The key is in my hand, I want to test everything, I want to know it all. I know what is good for me." So, we think ourselves masters, not servants, and from the position of a master we make our inquiry.

But this calculating mentality must be given up if we at all want to enter into the domain of the Lord, where everything is superior to us. No one there will care to come to us with an explanation, thinking that we are their master. They will not reassure us by saying, "Yes, there will be no loss; your gain will be big." We may think, "I am an independent separate entity, so in my account there must be no loss. I must stand here with my head erect," but that won't do. We are to go there as slaves, not masters. That sort of mentality is necessary: we must bow down our heads, not that with our heads erect we will march over everything. But everything there is superior in quality to us.

## DIVINE SLAVERY

So, we have to enter into that transcendental land, where even the earth, water, air, and whatever we will find, is made of higher materials than we ourselves are made of. They are all *guru*, and we are disciples. They are all masters, and we are servants; we have to enter the land where everything is our master. We will have to submit; that will be our real qualification. What we will be ordered to do, we will have to do. We are not to exercise our brain so much there. The brain has no room there; they are all brainier than we. Our brain is unnecessary there; only our hands are necessary. Menial labor is necessary there. Brain there is enough. We are to enter that land if we like. It is a land of slavery for us. So, we are to hatefully dismiss our brains, and taking only our hearts, we must approach and enter that land.

We should think, "I am as insignificant as a mosquito," just as Lord Brahmā did when he went to Dwārakā to visit Lord Krishna. And it is not only for the time being; not that one will accept a humble attitude, finish his work and then come back. No. We will have to accept such an insignificant position eternally. Of course, we may expect to be educated about Krishna consciousness: how it is good, how it is great, how it is useful to us. We will be allowed *paripraśna*, honest inquiry. In the transcendental realm, everyone is our friend. They will come to help us, to make us understand that devotional service is beautiful, and that Krishna consciousness is the best form of life. Our aspiration and purity of purpose is to be valued, not our external position. The recruiters from that side will consider our purity of purpose, not so much our present position and capacity.

And although apparently it seems that we are going to be slaves, the result is just the opposite. If you can accept such an attitude of surrender and slavery, then

He who can never be conquered, will be conquered. Friends will come and help you; the *sādhus* will come and make you understand that we should become slaves, that Krishna likes His slaves very much. He is the master of slaves, and sometimes He wants to become the slave of His slaves (*gopī-bhartuḥ pada-kamalayor dāsa-dāsānudāsaḥ*). This is the key to success, and we can achieve the highest gain through this attitude.

Śrī Chaitanya Mahāprabhu told Rāmānanda Rāya, "Yes, this is true. The unconquerable is conquered by surrender. We can capture Him. I accept this as the beginning plane of divine love: by giving we can get as much as we risk. As much as we risk to give ourselves, so much we can demand from that unconquerable infinite." Śrī Chaitanya Mahāprabhu said, "I accept this as the beginning of *śuddha-bhakti*, pure devotional service. But go farther."

## THE SCIENCE OF RASA

Rāmānanda Rāya explained that from there pure devotional service develops in a crude form, in a general way. And when it is more mature, it must take the shape of *śānta*, neutrality; *dāsya*, servitorship; *sakhya*, friendship; *vātsalya*, paternal affection; and *mādhurya rasa*, conjugal love. In *śānta rasa*, there is adherence, *niṣṭhā*; one thinks, "I cannot withdraw myself from this consciousness of continuous submission to the truth.

Neutrality develops into *dāsya rasa*, the desire to do some service. When a devotee is not satisfied by only sitting, showing loyalty to the Supreme Authority, he wants to be utilized by Him. He awaits the Lord's order, praying that the Lord may give him some engagement. When a devotee has such deep penetration that he wants to be utilized in any way by the Lord, that is known as *dāsya rasa*, or devotion in the mood of service. Then there *is sakhya rasa*; devotional service in friendship.

### GOD THE FRIEND

When, in *dāsya rasa*, confidence is added to service, then it becomes a little superior. Generally old servants who are faithful become confidential servants, so when the confidential stage is added to service, it becomes *sakhya rasa*, or devotional service as a friend of the Lord. First there is *niṣṭhā*, adherence, submission; then the devotee wants to be utilized for His satisfaction; then there is confidential utilization; and then it comes to friendly service, *sakhya rasa*. In Vaikuṇṭha, where Lord Nārāyaṇa is served in calculative devotion, only *śānta rasa*, *dāsya rasa*, and half of *sakhya rasa* are seen. Full confidence is not possible there. Awe, reverence, splendor, grandeur, pomp, apprehension—all these vanish when we develop a more confidential relationship with the Supreme Lord. At that time, the object of our worship or love changes in another way.

Then from Vaikuṇṭha, we feel attraction for Ayodhyā, the divine abode of Lord Rāmacandra, where there is neutrality, servitorship, and friendship with Vibhīṣaṇa and Sugrīva. There, we can also trace *vātsalya rasa*, parental love of Godhead.

## God the Son

In *vātsalya rasa*, confidence has developed to the peculiar stage in which the servitors think themselves promoted to the post of protecting the object of their veneration. Filial affection is also service. Although it seems that the parents are masters of the situation, controlling the Lord as their son, sometimes chastising and punishing Him, this is a superficial view. If we can enter into the depth of their service, we shall find an incomparable love of a most peculiar type. On the surface, they are engaged in punishing and rebuking the Lord; underground, they are full of interest for the welfare of the object of their service. *Vātsalya*, or parental love of Godhead, is a peculiar type of divine love. We see a very light type of *vātsalya* in Ayodhyā, so it is almost ignored.

## Mathurā: The Krishna Conception

Rūpa Goswāmī leaped from Vaikuṇṭha to Mathurā in one stride. In his *Upadeśamṛta* (9), he writes: *vaikuṇṭhaj janito varā madhu-purī tatrāpi rāsotsavād*. "Mathurā is superior to Vaikuṇṭha because Lord Śrī

Krishna appeared there." It is there that everything is shown in a clear and substantial way. In Mathurā we find the Krishna conception of Godhead. In one stride he has come from Vaikuṇṭha to the Krishna conception, but Sanātana Goswāmī has filled up the gap. In his book, *Bṛhad-bhāgavatāmṛta*, he says that on the way to Mathurā there is Ayodhyā, the spiritual kingdom of Lord Rāma, and there we find *sakhya* and *vātsalya rasa.*

But Rūpa Goswāmī goes to Mathurā at once. He says, "Come to Mathurā; here you will find *sakhya* and *vātsalya rasa* clearly visible. He has shown how *sakhya rasa* service is present there. The devotees there are playing with Krishna, sometimes climbing on His shoulders, and perhaps sometimes even giving Him a slap. But although they may mix with Him in this way, their heart is full of a peculiar type of service attitude. That is the criterion; they may give up their lives a thousand times to take a thorn out of His sole. They can sacrifice themselves a thousand times for the slightest satisfaction of their friend. They consider Him a thousand times more valuable than their own life. In *vātsalya rasa* also, the criterion is similar. For the slightest interest of the object of their veneration they can give their lives millions of times. Such affection is found there.

And then, from *vātsalya*, it progresses to conjugal love *(mādhurya rasa)*, the all-comprehensive *rasa* which includes adherence *(śānta-niṣṭhā)*, service *(dāsya)*, friendly confidence (*sakhya*), and parental love (*vātsalya rasa*). But the wholesale dedication of every atom of our existence for Krishna's satisfaction is found in *mādhurya rasa*, which includes all other *rasas*.

## PARAMOUR LOVE

And *mādhurya rasa* is more enhanced when it is couched in the form of *parakīya*, or paramour relationship. In *parakīya rasa*, the *gopīs* risk everything for the service of Krishna. *Parakīya rasa* takes two forms: in one, there is no obligation of anything; the union may happen or may not happen. So, because their meeting is very rare, it becomes even sweeter. There is another kind of *parakīya rasa*: we are told that ordinary food is not palatable to Krishna, but when He takes food by stealing, that is more tasteful to Him. If we can follow this art, that may also be applied in the case of *parakīya rasa*. "I am deceiving the party, getting what I want. I am stealing the property of someone else." That sort of posing becomes more tasteful to the subjective party.

And the dedicated party risks everything: their good name, society, future, and even the dictation of the religious scriptures. They take a wholesale risk, just as one time, when we were in Madras, the King of Jaipur gave some money for the construction of a temple. The money was sent to our head office in Calcutta. Out of five thousand rupees, the first installment was one thousand rupees, and the construction work was begun by sending a worker from our main center. Then, Mādhava Mahārāj and I were sent to Madras, where we heard that the king would soon come. In order to show him that some work had been done we raised the construction to some extent, so the king could be told, "Your money has been spent, and now the next installment is necessary." In order to do this, we incurred a debt. We took a loan for bricks and other things and raised the construction to a higher level.

When we wrote this to our *guru mahārāj*, we had some apprehension that he would chastise us, "Why have you taken this loan?" Instead of that, he gave us his appreciation. "You have risked your future in the service of Krishna. You have taken a loan, and that means you have to pay off that loan, so you have engaged your future energy in the service of Krishna. You will have to collect money and pay off the loan, so there is service with risk for the future." The *gopīs* consciously risked their future: "We have disobeyed our superior persons and the directions of the *Vedas*; what we do is neither approved by society, nor by the religious books. Our future is dark." Still, they could not but serve Krishna.

So, *vaikuṇṭhāj janito varā madhu-purī tatrāpi rāsotsavād*. *Janito* means *vātsalya rasa*, and *mādhurya rasa* in Vṛndāvana: *rādhā-kuṇḍam ihāpi gokula-pateḥ*. In the *mādhurya rasa* also, three groups are shown: Vṛndāvana in general, selected groups in Govardhana, and the highest group in Rādhā-kuṇḍa. All these things have been shown in the conversation between Rāmānanda Rāya and Śrī Chaitanya Mahāprabhu.

## RĀDHĀ: QUEEN OF THE GOPĪS

After this, Śrī Chaitanya Mahāprabhu said, "Go further." Then, Rāmānanda Rāya began to explain the kind of service rendered by Rādhārāṇī in *mādhurya rasa*. Her devotional service is categorically higher than that of all the other *gopīs*. *Rādhām ādhāya hṛdaye tatyāja vraja-sundarīḥ* (*Gīta-govinda* 3.1 by Jayadeva Goswāmī). The whole group of *gopis* can be canceled for only one: Śrīmatī Rādhārāṇī. What peculiar type of service may come from Her? And Krishna, the Original Personality of Godhead (*svayam-rūpa)* is only by the side of Rādhārāṇī. By the side of other *gopīs*, that is *prābhava prakāśa*, a plenary expansion, not *svayam-rūpa*, the original form. Such is the quality of Śrīmatī Rādhārāṇī. We should show our highest reverence to this highest ideal of devotional service.

## RĀDHĀ-KRISHNA: UNION IN SEPARATION

Then the last question came from Śrī Chaitanya Mahāprabhu: "Can you think of anything more than this?" Then, Rāmānanda Rāya said, "You asked me to quote scripture to support whatever I say, but here I won't be able to quote scripture from anywhere. Still, I

Lord Śrī Krishna, ecstasy Himself and Śrīmatī Rādhārāṇī, the embodiment of ecstatic love of Godhead.

have a new feeling within me, and if You would like to know that, I can explain it to You." In this way, one song was composed by Rāmānanda Rāya. He introduced this song by saying, "Whether or not it will be pleasing to You, I do not know, but it seems to me that there is a stage which is even better than the meeting of Rādhā and Govinda." There is a stage where both of Them, the positive and negative are combined, no individual consciousness is clear, and one is searching another in self-forgetfulness. This searching of one party by the other is very strong and intense. This seems to be a more highly elevated love: union in separation. Rādhā and Govinda are so intense in Their search of one another that even They have no consciousness of whether They have each other. Rādhārāṇī sometimes experiences that even while Krishna is present before Her, She fears losing Him; that feeling becomes as intense as if She has lost Him. They are together, but the apprehension that one may lose the other makes their meeting intolerably painful, just as a mother is always alert about the safety of her son (*aniṣṭa-śaṅkīni bandhu-hṛdayāni bhavanti hi*). A mother thinks, "Oh, my son is out—is he in an accident?" This fear of separation is the symptom of deep love.

## ŚRĪ CHAITANYA AVATĀRA

Rāmānanda Raya's composition gave a hint about the divine appearance of Śrī Chaitanya Mahāprabhu in which both Rādhā and Govinda are combined, and it is as if they are unconscious of Their separate existence. One is searching the other. Krishna Himself is overflowing with the feelings of Rādhārāṇī, and They are so deeply embraced that one is lost in the other. Then, Śrī Chaitanya Mahāprabhu put His palm over the mouth of Rāmānanda Rāya, and told him, "No further." *Rasa-rāja mahābhāva–dui eka rūpa.* Lord Śrī Krishna is the fountainhead of all pleasure, and Śṛimatī Rādhārāṇī is the embodiment of ecstatic love of Godhead. These two forms are united as one in Śrī Chaitanya Mahāprabhu.

## RASARĀJA: ECSTASY HIMSELF

Mahāprabhu replied, "Oh, because you are a cent-per-cent devotee, wherever you cast your glance you see only Krishna, nothing else. The object of your interest is represented everywhere." Rāmānanda Rāya said, "My Lord, don't deceive me in this way. You have come here so graciously to purify this mean person, and if You act diplomatically now, it will not look well for You. I won't hear what You say; come out with Your real position. Who are You?" Mahāprabhu said, "By dint of your loving devotion, you can know everything in this world; nothing can be concealed from your loving eye." *Premāñjana-cchurita-bhakti-vilocanena.*

Then, Mahāprabhu revealed Himself: "When you see Me to be externally of a golden color, it is not so. It is by the touch of the color of Rādhārāṇī. And who can Rādhārāṇī touch and closely embrace? She will never touch anyone except Krishna. So, now you know who I am: Rasarāja— ecstasy Himself, and Mahābhāva —the one who can taste that highest *rasa*. See how They mingle together!

Rāmānanda Rāya fainted and fell flat on the floor. He could not keep his senses. Then by the touch of His hand, Śrī Chaitanya Mahāprabhu again brought him to his senses. Rāmānanda returned to his previous stage of consciousness and saw a *sannyāsī* sitting before him. After a short pause, Mahāprabhu said, "Remain here, I am going."

Afterwards, Rāmānanda Rāya and Śrī Chaitanya Mahāprabhu had some other talks, and Mahāprabhu said, "Rāmānanda, as long as I live I want your company." Rāmānanda replied, "Yes, I must take shelter of Your divine feet and live there for the rest of my life." Rāmānanda later made arrangements with the King of Orissa to retire from his post as Governor of Madras and came to Jagannāth Purī. For almost two years, Śrī Chaitanya Mahāprabhu wandered about the holy places of Southern and Western India and at last returned to Purī. There they again met.

## TRANSCENDENTAL MADNESS

After this, Mahāprabhu went to Vṛndāvana through Bengal. Six years passed, and Advaita Prabhu almost gave leave to Mahāprabhu, saying, "Our pastimes of introducing the chanting of Hare Krishna are finished." Then Mahāprabhu continuously showed Rādhārāṇī's mood of tasting *krishna-prema*, ecstatic love of Krishna, for twelve years. Svarūpa Dāmodara and Rāmānanda Rāya, who are Lalitā and Viśākhā, the two principle *gopī*

An Orissan relief of Śrī Chaitanya Mahāprabhu and his two intimate associates, Rāmānanda Rāya and Svarupa Damodara. They assisted Mahāprabhu in tasting ecstatic love of Krishna during the last twelve years of His manifest pastimes.

assistants of Rādhārāṇī, were Mahāprabhu's most important company during that time. There, so many things about the deep feelings of Divine love have been shown. It has never been found in the history of the world, or even expressed in any scripture how such intense love within can produce such corresponding symptoms on the surface. That was shown by Rādhārāṇī and later shown by Śrī Chaitanya Mahāprabhu.

It was shown by Mahāprabhu in His practices also, how *krishna prema*, love of Krishna, can play a man like a doll. Sometimes His legs and hands would enter inconceivably into His body, and sometimes His joints would disconnect and His transcendental body would appear elongated. Sometimes His whole body would become white, and He would lay unconscious, breathing so slowly that His breath could not be traced. In this way, He exhibited many amazing symptoms of ecstasy.

Svarūpa Dāmodara, the personal secretary of Śrī Chaitanya Mahāprabhu has explained the meaning of His appearance in his memoirs, which were recorded in the *Chaitanya-caritāmṛta* of Kavirāj Goswāmī. He writes:

**rādhā kṛṣṇa-praṇaya-vikṛtir hlādinī śaktir asmād**
**ekātmānāv api bhuvi purā deha-bhedaṁ gatau tau**
**caitanyākhyaṁ prakaṭam adhunā tad-dvayaṁ caikyam āptaṁ**
**rādhā-bhāva-dyuti-suvalitaṁ naumi kṛṣṇa-svarūpam**

Sometimes Rādhā and Krishna are combined; sometimes They are separate. They are separate in Dvāpara-yuga, and in Kali-yuga they are combined as Śrī Krishna Chaitanya Mahāprabhu. Both are eternal expressions of the same Absolute Truth. Summer, autumn, winter, and spring continue in a cyclic order; it cannot be said that summer is the beginning and winter comes later. So, the pastimes of Śrī Rādhā and Krishna are eternally being enacted. In ancient times, sometimes Rādhā and Krishna divided Themselves and showed Their pastimes; again both of Them, the potency and the owner of the potency, are combined and closely embraced as Śrī Chaitanya Mahāprabhu. The predominating and the predominated moiety are mixed, and an extraordinary ecstatic feeling is there. Krishna is overpowered by His potency, and He Himself is

Śrī Chaitanya Mahāprabhu: Krishna Himself tasting His own internal sweetness and madly dancing in ecstasy. Krishna Himself is engaged in the search for Śrī Krishna, Reality the Beautiful.

searching after His own Self: *kṛṣṇasya ātmānusandhāna*. Krishna Himself is engaged in the search for Śrī Krishna, Reality the Beautiful. The influence of Rādhā-rāṇī over Krishna has transformed Him into a devotee, and He is searching Himself. Sweetness is tasting Itself and becoming mad. And it is living sweetness — not dead or static, but dynamic ecstasy, sweetness endowed with life. And He is tasting Himself, the personification of happiness, ecstasy, and beauty — and dancing in madness. And His performance of *kīrtan* means distributing that ecstasy to others. The ultimate sweetness, or *ānanda*, is such that no other thing exists that can taste itself and express its own happiness with such intensity. I have described Śrī Chaitanya Mahāprabhu in the *Prema Dhama Deva Stotram*:

**ātma-siddha-sāvalīlā-pūrṇa-saukhya-lakṣaṇaṁ**
**svānubhāva-matta-nṛtya-kīrttanātma-vaṇṭanam**
**advayaika-lakṣya-pūrṇa-tattva-tat-parātparaṁ**
**prema-dhāma-devam-eva naumi gaura-sundaram**

"The highest conception of the Absolute Truth must also be the highest form of *ānanda*, ecstasy. Mahāprabhu's dancing indicates that He is full of ecstasy, and His *kīrtan is* distribution of that *rasa*. So, if we scientifically search out who Mahāprabhu is, we cannot but find that He is the Ultimate Reality. He is mad in tasting His own internal nectar, and His dancing is the outcome of His transcendental ecstasy. And He is chanting, distributing that to others. So, studying quite closely the character of Śrī Chaitanya Mahāprabhu, we cannot but think that He is the Supreme Absolute Truth, in its fullest, and most dynamic expression."

# Explanation of the Logo of Sri Chaitanya Saraswat Math

*by His Divine Grace*
*Śrīla Bhakti Sundar Govinda Dev-Goswāmī Mahārāj*

*Oṁ* is the very gist of *Gāyatrī*, and from that *Oṁ* comes merciful rays, like the rays of the sun. Śrī Chaitanya Sāraswat Maṭh, where *saṅkīrtan* is always going on, is inside the flute of Krishna, and from there comes this sound *Oṁ*. *Oṁ*, the meaning of *Gāyatrī*, is coming from the Śrī Chaitanya Sāraswat Maṭh, and from there the explanation of *Gāyatrī* has been given by Śrīla B.R. Śrīdhar Dev-Goswāmī Mahārāj:

**gāyatrī muralīṣṭa-kīrttana-dhanaṁ rādhā-padaṁ dhīmahi**

The position of the *guru* is like water; the servitors of Śrī Chaitanya Sāraswat Maṭh are like lotuses; and the position of the worshipful Supreme Personality of Godhead is the Divine form of Rādhā-Krishna, *Oṁ*.

Everything is within *Oṁ*. *Oṁ* is coming from the flute of Krishna, and the meaning of *Oṁ*, of *Gāyatrī*, is *gāyatrī muralīṣṭa-kīrttana-dhanaṁ rādhā-padaṁ dhīmahi*. Krishna's flute does not make any other sound except the glorification of Śrīmatī Rādhārāṇī, and that is the real meaning and gist of the *Gāyatrī-Mantram*.

The sun's merciful rays give nourishment to the lotus, but if there is no water—if one cannot take shelter of Śrī Guru and His grace—then the lotus will become burnt by the rays of the sun.

Made in the USA
Monee, IL
13 July 2021

73498433R00115